SHAKESPEARE'S
Great
Soliloquies

SHAKESPEARE'S
Great
Soliloquies

WILLIAM SHAKESPEARE

EDITED BY
BOB BLAISDELL

DOVER PUBLICATIONS, INC.
MINEOLA, NEW YORK

To Kathy and Daniel
—B.B.

Bibliographical Note

Shakespeare's Great Soliloquies is a new work, first published by Dover Publications, Inc., in 2006. An introductory Note and brief contextual plot summaries, written by Bob Blaisdell, have been specially prepared for the present edition.

International Standard Book Number
ISBN-13: 978-0-486-44940-1
ISBN-10: 0-486-44940-8

Manufactured in the United States by LSC Communications
44940806   2016
www.doverpublications.com

NOTE

DEPENDING on how "soliloquy" is defined and how it was applied and understood by Shakespeare as he wrote the plays, there exist two or three times as many soliloquies as the hundred-and-five in this volume. We remember situation after situation in Shakespeare's plays where characters who believe themselves alone speak of their dilemmas, their loves, their schemes, their furies; sometimes, unfortunately or fortunately as the case may be, they are overheard or, becoming aware of the entrance of someone, lower their voices or even stop talking altogether. Shakespeare's soliloquizing characters do not *think* their private speeches aloud, they *speak* them. As Professor James Hirsh has shown, neatly and exhaustively, "In Shakespeare's plays soliloquies are self-addressed speeches, not short-cuts to the essential being of a character or direct representation of the character's thoughts, but rather examples of outward behavior that we must interpret, along with the character's other outward behavior."[1] So the majority of these soliloquies are addresses by characters to themselves when they believe themselves to be alone (exceptions include Lear's stormy night on the heath and Juliet's address to the night, both of which might properly be called *apostrophes*).

Most of us have seen Shakespeare's soliloquies performed as if the character is not speaking, but thinking: that is, we witness an interior monologue; we also occasionally see the soliloquies performed as if the character is aware of us in our seats and blithely shares his thoughts with us. These examples, however, are directorial decisions about how to perform Shakespeare rather than representations of how Elizabethan audiences and Shakespeare

---

[1] James Hirsh. *Shakespeare and the History of Soliloquies.* Fairleigh Dickinson University Press. 2003. 29.

himself would have understood the plays. In Shakespeare's heyday in the late sixteenth and early seventeenth centuries the fashion of characters addressing audiences was over (thus, part of the comedy of the buffoons performing the interlude "Pyramus and Thisby" in *A Midsummer Night's Dream* is that, unaware of the new convention of play-acting, they call out explanations and reassurances to their wedding-day audience), and as yet there were no such things in European theater as interior monologues.

In thinking about these characters and these moments in the plays, then, it is essential to realize as much of the context (behind and ahead) as possible. We must know Othello when he is *not* plagued by jealousy to understand him when it has driven him to murder, and we must be familiar with Lady Macbeth's relationship to her husband before we can very well interpret her guiding hand in her husband's murder of the king. I have introduced each soliloquy with the briefest of contextual summary to remind readers of the situation and the motivations of the character, but there is no substitute, of course, for reading and rereading the play. (As Samuel Johnson, the bard's most sensible editor, says in his "Preface to Shakespeare": ". . . his real power is not shown in the splendour of particular passages, but by the progress of his fable, and the tenour of his dialogue; and he that tries to recommend him by select quotations, will succeed like the pedant in *Hierocles*, who, when he offered his house to sale, carried a brick in his pocket as a specimen.") The soliloquies are arranged alphabetically by play, listed by the common rather than full title (not "The Life of King Henry the Fifth" but "Henry V"). The texts come from various standard editions, emended only for some consistency in punctuation.

For historical information about and persuasive discussion of how Shakespeare and his audiences comprehended soliloquies, the best, most interesting book, quoted above, is Hirsh's *Shakespeare and the History of Soliloquies*. Other studies include Morris Arnold's *The Soliloquies of Shakespeare* (Columbia University Press, 1911) and Wolfgang Clemen's *Shakespeare's Soliloquies* (Methuen, 1987). Particularly helpful for preparing actors for Shakespeare's speeches, not necessarily soliloquies, is the delightful *Speak the Speech! Shakespeare's Monologues Illuminated*, by Rhona Silverbush and Sami Plotkin (Faber and Faber, 2002). Finally I thank my friend the actress Katherine Hiler for suggesting several of the selections and for her advice on the introductory notes.

Contents

Hamlet

Henry IV, Part 1

Henry IV, Part 2

Henry V

Henry VI, Part 1

Henry VI, Part 2

Love's Labour's Lost

Macbeth

Measure for Measure

The Merry Wives of Windsor

A Midsummer Night's Dream

ALL'S WELL THAT ENDS WELL

Helena: "O, were that all! I think not on my father"
[Act I, Scene 1]

{*Helena is the daughter of Gerard de Narbon, the renown physician of the Countess of Rossillion who has died recently. Having been comforted by friends about her father's death, she finds more troubling her situation that, as the countess's ward, she is in love with the countess's son, Bertram, the new Duke of Rossillion, who in his new responsibilities is setting off for the French court.*}

O, were that all! I think not on my father,
And these great tears grace his remembrance more
Than those I shed for him. What was he like?
I have forgot him. My imagination
Carries no favor in't but Bertram's.
I am undone; there is no living, none,
If Bertram be away. 'Twere all one
That I should love a bright particular star
And think to wed it, he is so above me.
In his bright radiance and collateral light
Must I be comforted, not in his sphere.
Th' ambition in my love thus plagues itself:
The hind that would be mated by the lion
Must die for love. 'Twas pretty, though a plague,
To see him every hour; to sit and draw
His archèd brows, his hawking eye, his curls,
In our heart's table—heart too capable
Of every line and trick of his sweet favour.
But now he's gone, and my idolatrous fancy
Must sanctify his relics.

Helena: "Our remedies oft in ourselves do lie"
[Act I, Scene 1]

{*In the same scene as the previous, Helena hopes to prove her worthiness of Bertram by using what her father taught her about medicine and healing the King's apparently fatal fistula.*}

Our remedies oft in ourselves do lie,
Which we ascribe to heaven. The fated sky
Gives us free scope; only doth backward pull
Our slow designs when we ourselves are dull.
What power is it which mounts my love so high,
That makes me see, and cannot feed mine eye?
The mightiest space in fortune nature brings
To join like likes, and kiss like native things.
Impossible be strange attempts to those
That weigh their pains in sense, and do suppose
What hath been cannot be. Who ever strove
To show her merit that did miss her love?
The king's disease—my project may deceive me,
But my intents are fix'd, and will not leave me.

ANTONY AND CLEOPATRA

Enobarbus: "I am alone the villain of the earth"
[Act IV, Scene 6]

{*Domitius Enobarbus, one of Antony's friends, has gone over to the side of Octavius Caesar, Antony's rival triumvir. Antony, preparing to fight Caesar, understands his friend's decision, and has sent to Enobarbus his share of bounty from the campaigns they shared.*}

I am alone the villain of the earth,
And feel I am so most. O Antony,
Thou mine of bounty, how wouldst thou have paid
My better service, when my turpitude
Thou dost so crown with gold! This blows my heart.
If swift thought break it not, a swifter mean
Shall outstrike thought; but thought will do't, I feel.
I fight against thee? No! I will go seek
Some ditch wherein to die; the foul'st best fits
My latter part of life.

Enobarbus: "O, bear me witness, night—" [Act IV, Scene 9]

{*Enobarbus, having found "some ditch wherein to die," is broken-hearted on the night before Caesar's battle with Antony. He is observed during this fatal soliloquy by patrolling sentries who "stand close, and list him."*}

O, bear me witness, night—
Be witness to me, O thou blessèd moon,
When men revolted shall upon record

Bear hateful memory, poor Enobarbus did
Before thy face repent!
O sovereign mistress of true melancholy,
The poisonous damp of night disponge upon me,
That life, a very rebel to my will,
May hang no longer on me. Throw my heart
Against the flint and hardness of my fault,
Which, being dried with grief, will break to powder,
And finish all foul thoughts. O Antony,
Nobler than my revolt is infamous,
Forgive me in thine own particular,
But let the world rank me in register
A master-leaver and a fugitive!
O Antony! O Antony!

[*He dies.*]

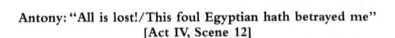

Antony: "All is lost!/This foul Egyptian hath betrayed me" [Act IV, Scene 12]

{*Antony, having lost in an ill-conceived sea battle against Caesar, has cursed his lover Cleopatra, who he believes has betrayed him by suggesting this battle. The bracketed ellipsis [. . .] indicates an interruption in the soliloquy, where Antony gives orders to and addresses his lieutenant.*}

All is lost!
This foul Egyptian hath betrayed me.
My fleet hath yielded to the foe, and yonder
They cast their caps up and carouse together
Like friends long lost. Triple-turn'd whore! 'Tis thou
Hast sold me to this novice; and my heart
Makes only wars on thee. [. . .]
O sun, thy uprise shall I see no more!
Fortune and Antony part here; even here
Do we shake hands. All come to this? The hearts
That spaniel'd me at heels, to whom I gave
Their wishes, do discandy, melt their sweets
On blossoming Caesar; and this pine is bark'd
That overtopp'd them all. Betray'd I am.

O this false soul of Egypt! this grave charm,
Whose eye beck'd forth my wars, and call'd them home,
Whose bosom was my crownet, my chief end,
Like a right gypsy hath at fast and loose
Beguil'd me to the very heart of loss.

Cleopatra: "I dreamt there was an Emperor Antony" [Act V, Scene 2]

{*Cleopatra has witnessed Antony's death, the result of his despairing suicide. Attended by one of Caesar's men, Dolabella, who tries to interrupt her in the course of the speech, the captured queen of Egypt seems to be speaking to herself from the clouds of her sleep.*}

I dreamt there was an Emperor Antony.
O, such another sleep, that I might see
But such another man!
His face was as the heav'ns, and therein stuck
A sun and moon, which kept their course and lighted
The little O, th' earth.
His legs bestrid the ocean; his rear'd arm
Crested the world. His voice was propertied
As all the tunèd spheres, and that to friends;
But when he meant to quail and shake the orb,
He was as rattling thunder. For his bounty,
There was no winter in't; an autumn 'twas
That grew the more by reaping. His delights
Were dolphin-like: they show'd his back above
The element they liv'd in. In his livery
Walk'd crowns and crownets; realms and islands were
As plates dropp'd from his pocket.

AS YOU LIKE IT

Orlando: "Hang there, my verse, in witness of my love"
[Act III, Scene 2]

{*A young man in love with Rosalind, a banished duke's daughter, Orlando is forced by his wicked older brother to flee for his life into the same forest where Rosalind and her father are hiding. There, among the trees, Orlando posts his poems proclaiming his love.*}

Hang there, my verse, in witness of my love;
And thou, thrice-crownèd Queen of Night, survey
With thy chaste eye, from thy pale sphere above,
Thy huntress' name that my full life doth sway.
O Rosalind! these trees shall be my books,
And in their barks my thoughts I'll character,
That every eye which in this forest looks
Shall see thy virtue witness'd everywhere.
Run, run, Orlando; carve on every tree,
The fair, the chaste, and unexpressive she.

CORIOLANUS

Coriolanus: "Most sweet voices!/Better it is to die, better to starve" [Act II, Scene 3]

{Having defeated the Volscians, Coriolanus, the military hero of Rome, is bitter that the citizens of Rome demand his humbling himself to them before they will elect him consul.}

Most sweet voices!
Better it is to die, better to starve,
Than crave the hire which first we do deserve.
Why in this woolvish toge should I stand here,
To beg of Hob and Dick, that do appear,
Their needless vouches? Custom calls me to't.
What custom wills, in all things should we do't,
The dust on antique time would lie unswept,
And mountainous error be too highly heapt
For truth to o'er-peer. Rather than fool it so,
Let the high office and the honour go
To one that would do thus. I am half through;
The one part suffer'd, the other will I do.

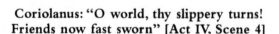

Coriolanus: "O world, thy slippery turns! Friends now fast sworn" [Act IV, Scene 4]

{Having thrown off the shackles of political expediency, Coriolanus "banishes" Rome for having banished him, and decides to go to Antium to offer his services to his old enemy, the Volscians' leader Tullus Aufidius.}

O world, thy slippery turns! Friends now fast sworn,
Whose double bosoms seem to wear one heart,

Whose hours, whose bed, whose meal, and exercise,
Are still together; who twin, as 'twere, in love
Unseparable, shall within this hour,
On a dissension of a doit, break out
To bitterest enmity: so, fellest foes,
Whose passions and whose plots have broke their sleep,
To take the one the other, by some chance,
Some trick not worth an egg, shall grow dear friends
And interjoin their issues. So with me:
My birthplace hate I, and my love's upon
This enemy town. I'll enter: if he slay me,
He does fair justice; if he give me way,
I'll do his country service.

CYMBELINE

**Posthumus: "O noble misery!/To be i' the field, and ask,
'What news?' of me!" [Act V, Scene 3]**

{*Believing his wife Imogen has been killed by his own order, a result of his un-
founded jealousy, Posthumus gives up his decision to fight with Rome against
Cymbeline, King of Britain, Imogen's father.*}

O noble misery!
To be i' the field, and ask, "What news?" of me!
Today how many would have given their honours
To have saved their carcasses, took heel to do't,
And yet died too! I, in mine own woe charm'd,
Could not find death where I did hear him groan,
Nor feel him where he struck: being an ugly monster,
'Tis strange he hides him in fresh cups, soft beds,
Sweet words; or hath more ministers than we
That draw his knives i' the war. Well, I will find him
For being now a favourer to the Briton,
No more a Briton. I have resumed again
The part I came in. Fight I will no more,
But yield me to the veriest hind that shall
Once touch my shoulder. Great the slaughter is
Here made by the Roman; great the answer be
Britons must take. For me, my ransom's death.
On either side I come to spend my breath,
Which neither here I'll keep nor bear again,
But end it by some means for Imogen.

Posthumus: "Sleep, thou hast been a grandsire, and begot" [Act V, Scene 4]

{In remorse for his ordered execution of Imogen (he does not know the order was not carried out), Posthumus has allowed himself to be taken captive by the Britons. He dreams in his cell of his dead father, mother, and brothers, and finally of the god Jupiter, who in fact leaves him with a written tablet on his chest. Posthumus awakens and reflects.}

Sleep, thou hast been a grandsire, and begot
A father to me; and thou hast created
A mother and two brothers: but, O scorn!
Gone! they went hence so soon as they were born:
And so I am awake. Poor wretches that depend
On greatness' favour dream as I have done,
Wake, and find nothing. But, alas, I swerve:
Many dream not to find, neither deserve,
And yet are steep'd in favours. So am I,
That have this golden chance and know not why.
What fairies haunt this ground? A book? O rare one!
Be not, as is our fangled world, a garment
Nobler than that it covers. Let thy effects
So follow, to be most unlike our courtiers,
As good as promise.
[*Reads.*]

"When as a lion's whelp shall, to himself unknown, without seeking find, and be embraced by a piece of tender air; and when from a stately cedar shall be lopped branches which, being dead many years, shall after revive, be jointed to the old stock, and freshly grow; then shall Posthumus end his miseries, Britain be fortunate and flourish in peace and plenty."

'Tis still a dream, or else such stuff as madmen
Tongue, and brain not; either both or nothing;
Or senseless speaking or a speaking such
As sense cannot untie. Be what it is,
The action of my life is like it, which
I'll keep, if but for sympathy.

HAMLET

Hamlet: "Now I am alone./O, what a rogue
and peasant slave am I!" [Act II, Scene 2]

{*Hamlet, Prince of Denmark, burning to avenge his uncle's murder of his
father, reflects on the actor's ability to simulate grief while he, Hamlet, with real
grief, can neither show it nor take measures about it. He concocts a plan to
allow actors to expose his uncle's guilt.*}

Now I am alone.
O, what a rogue and peasant slave am I!
Is it not monstrous that this player here,
But in a fiction, in a dream of passion,
Could force his soul so to his own conceit
That from her working all his visage wann'd,
Tears in his eyes, distraction in 's aspect,
A broken voice, and his whole function suiting
With forms to his conceit? and all for nothing!
For Hecuba!
What's Hecuba to him, or he to Hecuba,
That he should weep for her? What would he do
Had he the motive and the cue for passion
That I have? He would drown the stage with tears,
And cleave the general ear with horrid speech,
Make mad the guilty and appal the free,
Confound the ignorant, and amaze indeed
The very faculties of eyes and ears.
Yet I,
A dull and muddy-mettled rascal, peak,
Like John-a-dreams, unpregnant of my cause,
And can say nothing; no, not for a king,
Upon whose property and most dear life

11

A damn'd defeat was made. Am I a coward?
Who calls me villain? breaks my pate across?
Plucks off my beard, and blows it in my face?
Tweaks me by the nose? gives me the lie i' the throat,
As deep as to the lungs? who does me this?
Ha!
'Swounds, I should take it, for it cannot be
But I am pigeon-liver'd and lack gall
To make oppression bitter, or ere this
I should have fatted all the region kites
With this slave's offal: bloody, bawdy villain!
Remorseless, treacherous, lecherous, kindless villain!
O, vengeance!
Why, what an ass am I! This is most brave,
That I, the son of a dear father murder'd,
Prompted to my revenge by heaven and hell,
Must, like a whore, unpack my heart with words,
And fall a-cursing, like a very drab,
A scullion!
Fie upon't! foh! About, my brain! I have heard
That guilty creatures sitting at a play
Have by the very cunning of the scene
Been struck so to the soul that presently
They have proclaim'd their malefactions;
For murder, though it have no tongue, will speak
With most miraculous organ. I'll have these players
Play something like the murder of my father
Before mine uncle; I'll observe his looks;
I'll tent him to the quick: if he but blench,
I know my course. The spirit that I have seen
May be the devil: and the devil hath power
To assume a pleasing shape; yea, and perhaps
Out of my weakness and my melancholy,
As he is very potent with such spirits,
Abuses me to damn me. I'll have grounds
More relative than this: the play's the thing
Wherein I'll catch the conscience of the king.

Hamlet: "To be or not to be, that is the question"
[Act III, Scene 1]

{*Hamlet, still undecided on which actions to take against his murderous uncle (and, perhaps, simulating this soliloquy for the purpose of deceiving King Claudius's spies), contemplates the arguments for and against continuing one's life of misery and suffering.*}

To be or not to be, that is the question:
Whether 'tis nobler in the mind to suffer
The slings and arrows of outrageous fortune,
Or to take arms against a sea of troubles,
And by opposing end them? To die: to sleep;
No more; and by a sleep to say we end
The heartache and the thousand natural shocks
That flesh is heir to, 'tis a consummation
Devoutly to be wish'd. To die, to sleep;
To sleep: perchance to dream: ay, there's the rub;
For in that sleep of death what dreams may come
When we have shuffled off this mortal coil,
Must give us pause. There's the respect
That makes calamity of so long life;
For who would bear the whips and scorns of time,
The oppressor's wrong, the proud man's contumely,
The pangs of dispriz'd love, the law's delay,
The insolence of office and the spurns
That patient merit of the unworthy takes,
When he himself might his quietus make
With a bare bodkin? Who would these fardels bear,
To grunt and sweat under a weary life,
But that the dread of something after death,
The undiscover'd country from whose bourn
No traveller returns, puzzles the will
And makes us rather bear those ills we have
Than fly to others that we know not of?
Thus conscience does make cowards of us all;
And thus the native hue of resolution
Is sicklied o'er with the pale cast of thought,
And enterprises of great pith and moment
With this regard their currents turn awry,

And lose the name of action.—Soft you now!
The fair Ophelia! Nymph, in thy orisons
Be all my sins remember'd.

Ophelia: "O, what a noble mind is here o'er-thrown!"
[Act III, Scene 1]

{*Ophelia, rejected and insulted by Hamlet, her former fiancé, wonders at his behavior.*}

O, what a noble mind is here o'er-thrown!
The courtier's, soldier's, scholar's eye, tongue, sword;
The expectancy and rose of the fair state,
The glass of fashion and the mould of form,
The observed of all observers, quite, quite down!
And I, of ladies most deject and wretched,
That suck'd the honey of his music vows,
Now see that noble and most sovereign reason,
Like sweet bells jangled, out of tune and harsh;
That unmatch'd form and feature of blown youth
Blasted with ecstasy: O! woe is me,
To have seen what I have seen, see what I see!

Hamlet: "'Tis now the very witching time of night"
[Act III, Scene 2]

{*Having satisfactorily exposed his uncle's guilt through the actors' entertainment, Hamlet prepares himself to confront his mother, whom he despises for having married his uncle.*}

'Tis now the very witching time of night,
When churchyards yawn and hell itself breathes out
Contagion to this world: now could I drink hot blood,
And do such bitter business as the day
Would quake to look on. Soft! now to my mother.
O heart! lose not thy nature; let not ever

The soul of Nero enter this firm bosom:
Let me be cruel, not unnatural:
I will speak daggers to her, but use none;
My tongue and soul in this be hypocrites;
How in my words soever she be shent,
To give them seals never, my soul, consent!

Claudius, King of Denmark: "O, my offence is rank, it smells to heaven!" [Act III, Scene 3]

{*Hamlet's guilty uncle Claudius, moved to repentance for his murder of his brother the king, prepares himself for prayer.*}

O, my offence is rank it smells to heaven!
It hath the primal eldest curse upon't,
A brother's murder! Pray can I not,
Though inclination be as sharp as will:
My stronger guilt defeats my strong intent;
And, like a man to double business bound,
I stand in pause where I shall first begin,
And both neglect. What if this cursed hand
Were thicker than itself with brother's blood,
Is there not rain enough in the sweet heavens
To wash it white as snow? Whereto serves mercy
But to confront the visage of offence?
And what's in prayer but this two-fold force,
To be forestalled ere we come to fall,
Or pardon'd being down? Then I'll look up;
My fault is past. But, O, what form of prayer
Can serve my turn? "Forgive me my foul murder"?
That cannot be; since I am still possess'd
Of those effects for which I did the murder:
My crown, mine own ambition, and my queen.
May one be pardon'd and retain the offence?
In the corrupted currents of this world
Offence's gilded hand may shove by justice,
And oft 'tis seen the wicked prize itself
Buys out the law; but 'tis not so above;

There is no shuffling, there the action lies
In his true nature, and we ourselves compell'd,
Even to the teeth and forehead of our faults
To give in evidence. What then? what rests?
Try what repentance can: what can it not?
Yet what can it, when one can not repent?
O wretched state! O bosom black as death!
O limèd soul, that, struggling to be free,
Art more engaged! Help, angels! Make assay!
Bow, stubborn knees; and, heart with strings of steel,
Be soft as sinews of the newborn babe!
All may be well.

HENRY IV, PART 1

Prince Hal: "I know you all, and will awhile uphold"
[Act I, Scene 2]

{*Prince Hal, King Henry IV's son, lives a dissolute life, mixing with clowns and no-goods (foremost among them Sir John Falstaff), much to the annoyance and displeasure of his father. A time will come, Hal now reflects, when to the surprise of the disappointed court, he will reform his ways.*}

I know you all, and will awhile uphold
The unyoked humour of your idleness:
Yet herein will I imitate the sun,
Who doth permit the base contagious clouds
To smother up his beauty from the world,
That, when he please again to be himself,
Being wanted, he may be more wonder'd at,
By breaking through the foul and ugly mists
Of vapours that did seem to strangle him.
If all the year were playing holidays,
To sport would be as tedious as to work;
But when they seldom come, they wish'd for come,
And nothing pleaseth but rare accidents.
So, when this loose behavior I throw off,
And pay the debt I never promised,
By how much better than my word I am,
By so much shall I falsify men's hopes;
And like bright metal on a sullen ground,
My reformation, glittering o'er my fault,
Shall show more goodly and attract more eyes
Than that which hath no foil to set it off.
I'll so offend, to make offence a skill;
Redeeming time when men think least I will.

Hotspur: "'But, for mine own part, my lord, I could be well contented . . .'" [Act II, Scene 3]

{*Henry Percy, known as "Hotspur," is the son of the Earl of Northumberland. He has fought for King Henry IV in Scotland, but now conspires with the enemy Douglas against the king and will attempt to launch a military attack. In this scene Hotspur has received a letter from a friend who refuses to join the rebellion.*}

"But for mine own part, my lord, I could be well contented to be there, in respect of the love I bear your house."

He could be contented: why is he not, then? In respect of the love he bears our house: he shows in this he loves his own barn better than he loves our house. Let me see some more.

"The purpose you undertake is dangerous;—"

Why, that's certain: 'tis dangerous to take a cold, to sleep, to drink; but I tell you, my lord fool, out of this nettle, danger, we pluck this flower, safety.

"The purpose you undertake is dangerous; the friends you have named uncertain; the time itself unsorted; and your whole plot too light for the counterpoise of so great an opposition."

Say you so, say you so? I say unto you again, you are a shallow cowardly hind, and you lie. What a lack-brain is this! By the Lord, our plot is a good plot as ever was laid; our friends true and constant: a good plot, good friends, and full of expectation; an excellent plot, very good friends. What a frosty-spirited rogue is this! Why, my lord of York commends the plot and the general course of action. Zounds! an I were now by this rascal, I could brain him with his lady's fan. Is there not my father, my uncle, and myself? Lord Edmund Mortimer, my Lord of York, and Owen Glendower? Is there not besides the Douglas? Have I not all their letters to meet me in arms by the ninth of the next month? And are they not some of them set forward already? What a pagan rascal is this! an infidel! Ha! You shall see now in very sincerity of fear and cold heart, will he to the king and lay open all our proceedings. O! I could divide myself and go to buffets, for moving such a dish of skim milk with so honourable an action! Hang him! Let him tell the king: we are prepared. I will set forward tonight.

Falstaff: "If I be not ashamed of my soldiers, I am a soused gurnet." [Act IV, Scene 2]

{*Sir John Falstaff, Prince Hal's lazy, self-indulgent, witty, cowardly friend, describes in a rare moment of self-reflection, how he has found himself in a pickle. By taking bribes from the capable, competent men, he has recruited in their stead a beggarly bunch.*}

If I be not ashamed of my soldiers, I am a soused gurnet. I have misused the king's press damnably. I have got, in exchange of a hundred and fifty soldiers, three hundred and odd pounds. I press me none but good householders, yeomen's sons; inquire me out contracted bachelors, such as had been asked twice on the banns; such a commodity of warm slaves, as had as lief hear the devil as a drum; such as fear the report of a caliver worse than a struck fowl or a hurt wild-duck. I pressed me none but such toasts-and-butter, with hearts in their bellies no bigger than pins' heads, and they have bought out their services; and now my whole charge consists of ancients, corporals, lieutenants, gentlemen of companies, slaves as ragged as Lazarus in the painted cloth, where the glutton's dogs licked his sores; and such as indeed were never soldiers, but discarded unjust serving-men, younger sons to younger brothers, revolted tapsters and ostlers trade-fallen, the cankers of a calm world and a long peace, ten times more dishonourable ragged than an old faced ancient: and such have I, to fill up the rooms of them that have bought out their services, that you would think that I had a hundred and fifty tattered prodigals lately come from swine-keeping, from eating draff and husks. A mad fellow met me on the way and told me I had unloaded all the gibbets and pressed the dead bodies. No eye hath seen such scarecrows. I'll not march through Coventry with them, that's flat: nay, and the villains march wide betwixt the legs, as if they had gyves on; for indeed I had the most of them out of prison. There's but a shirt and a half in all my company; and the half shirt is two napkins tacked together and thrown over the shoulders like an herald's coat without sleeves; and the shirt, to say the truth, stolen from my host at Saint Alban's, or the red-nose innkeeper of Daventry. But that's all one; they'll find linen enough on every hedge.

HENRY IV, PART 2

King Henry IV: "How many thousand of my poorest subjects" [Act III, Scene 1]

{*Having summoned his supporters, the Earls of Surrey and Warwick, to his room in his Westminster palace at one in the morning, the restless king, beset by a threatened civil war and an invasion by the French, rues his responsbilities.*}

How many thousand of my poorest subjects
Are at this hour asleep! O sleep! O gentle sleep!
Nature's soft nurse, how have I frighted thee,
That thou no more wilt weigh my eyelids down
And steep my senses in forgetfulness?
Why rather, sleep, liest thou in smoky cribs,
Upon uneasy pallets stretching thee,
And hush'd with buzzing night-flies to thy slumber,
Than in the perfum'd chambers of the great,
Under the canopies of costly state,
And lull'd with sound of sweetest melody?
O thou dull god! Why liest thou with the vile
In loathsome beds, and leav'st the kingly couch
A watch-case or a common 'larum-bell?
Wilt thou upon the high and giddy mast
Seal up the ship-boy's eyes, and rock his brains
In cradle of the rude imperious surge,
And in the visitation of the winds,
Who take the ruffian billows by the top,
Curling their monstrous heads and hanging them
With deaf'ning clamour in the slippery clouds,
That, with the hurly, death itself awakes?
Canst thou, O partial sleep, give thy repose
To the wet sea-boy in an hour so rude,

20

And in the calmest and most stillest night,
With all appliances and means to boot,
Deny it to a king? Then, happy low, lie down!
Uneasy lies the head that wears a crown.

Falstaff: "As I return, I will fetch off these justices . . ." [Act III, Scene 2]

{*In Gloucestershire, Falstaff has just met with Justice of the Peace Robert Shallow, a disreputable chum of Falstaff's from many years past, as Falstaff continues to recruit men for the king's army (and accept bribes for exempting others).*}

As I return, I will fetch off these justices: I do see the bottom of Justice Shallow. Lord, Lord! How subject we old men are to this vice of lying! This same starved justice hath done nothing but prate to me of the wildness of his youth and the feats he hath done about Turnbull Street: and every third word a lie, duer paid to the hearer than the Turk's tribute. I do remember him at Clement's Inn like a man made after supper of a cheese-paring: when a' was naked, he was, for all the world, like a forked radish, with a head fantastically carved upon it with a knife: a' was so forlorn that his dimensions to any thick sight were invincible: a' was the very genius of famine; yet lecherous as a monkey, and the whores called him mandrake: a' came ever in the rearward of the fashion, and sung those tunes to the overscutched huswives that he heard the carmen whistle, and sware they were his fancies or his good-nights. And now is this Vice's dagger become a squire, and talks as familiarly of John a Gaunt as if he had been sworn brother to him; and I'll be sworn a' ne'er saw him but once in the Tilt-yard; and then he burst his head for crowding among the marshal's men. I saw it, and told John a Gaunt he beat his own name; for you might have thrust him and all his apparel into an eel-skin; the case of a treble hautboy was a mansion for him, a court: and now has he land and beefs. Well, I will be acquainted with him, if I return; and it shall go hard but I will make him a philosopher's two stones to me. If the young dace be a bait for the old pike, I see no reason in the law of nature but I may snap at him. Let time shape, and there an end.

HENRY V

King Henry: "Upon the king! Let us our lives, our souls"
[Act IV, Scene 1]

{*Henry has been in disguise as a watchman in the English camp at Agincourt, mingling with his common soliders on the night before battle against the French. Appreciating their candor, he better understands his responsibilties as their king.*}

Upon the king! Let us our lives, our souls,
Our debts, our careful wives,
Our children and our sins lay on the king
We must bear all. O hard condition!
Twin-born with greatness, subject to the breath
Of every fool, whose sense no more can feel
But his own wringing. What infinite heart's ease
Must kings neglect that private men enjoy!
And what have kings that privates have not too,
Save ceremony, save general ceremony?
And what art thou, thou idle ceremony?
What kind of god art thou, that suffer'st more
Of mortal griefs than do thy worshippers?
What are thy rents? What are thy comings in?
O ceremony, show me but thy worth!
What is thy soul of adoration?
Art thou aught else but place, degree, and form,
Creating awe and fear in other men?
Wherein thou art less happy being fear'd
Than they in fearing.
What drink'st thou oft, instead of homage sweet,
But poison'd flattery? O, be sick, great greatness,
And bid thy ceremony give thee cure!

Think'st thou the fiery fever will go out
With titles blown from adulation?
Will it give place to flexure and low bending?
Canst thou, when thou command'st the beggar's knee,
Command the health of it? No, thou proud dream,
That play'st so subtly with a king's repose;
I am a king that find thee, and I know
'Tis not the balm, the sceptre and the ball,
The sword, the mace, the crown imperial,
The intertissued robe of gold and pearl,
The farced title running 'fore the king,
The throne he sits on, nor the tide of pomp
That beats upon the high shore of this world,
No, not all these, thrice-gorgeous ceremony,
Not all these, laid in bed majestical,
Can sleep so soundly as the wretched slave,
Who with a body fill'd and vacant mind
Gets him to rest, cramm'd with distressful bread;
Never sees horrid night, the child of hell,
But, like a lackey, from the rise to set,
Sweats in the eye of Phoebus and all night
Sleeps in Elysium; next day after dawn,
Doth rise and help Hyperion to his horse,
And follows so the ever-running year,
With profitable labour, to his grave:
And, but for ceremony, such a wretch,
Winding up days with toil and nights with sleep,
Had the fore-hand and vantage of a king.
The slave, a member of the country's peace,
Enjoys it; but in gross brain little wots
What watch the king keeps to maintain the peace,
Whose hours the peasant best advantages.

King Henry: "O God of battles, steel my soldiers' hearts"
[Act IV, Scene 1]

{*In the morning, following his night among the soldiers, Henry goes to meet his nobles. First, however, he offers a prayer and reflects on the expiations taken for his father's crimes against King Richard II.*}

O God of battles, steel my soldiers' hearts,
Possess them not with fear! Take from them now
The sense of reck'ning, if th' opposèd numbers
Pluck their hearts from them. Not today, O Lord!
O, not today, think not upon the fault
My father made in compassing the crown!
I Richard's body have interrèd new;
And on it have bestowed more contrite tears
Than from it issued forcèd drops of blood.
Five hundred poor I have in yearly pay,
Who twice a day their withered hands hold up
Toward heaven to pardon blood;
And I have built two chantries,
Where the sad and solemn priests sing still
For Richard's soul. More will I do:
Though all that I can do is nothing worth,
Since that my penitence comes after all,
Imploring pardon.

HENRY VI, PART 1

La Pucelle (Joan of Arc): "The regent conquers, and the Frenchmen fly" [Act V, Scene 3]

{*In the midst of a losing battle at Angiers in France, La Pucelle, better known to us as Joan of Arc, tries to rally support from her supernatural powers, "the Fiends." They refuse to help her any longer, and after her incantation, the Duke of York enters the field and duels and captures her.*}

The regent conquers, and the Frenchmen fly.
Now help, ye charming spells and periapts;
And ye choice spirits that admonish me
And give me signs of future accidents.

[*Thunder.*]

You speedy helpers, that are substitutes
Under the lordly monarch of the north,
Appear, and aid me in this enterprise.

[*Enter Fiends.*]

This speedy and quick appearance argues proof
Of your accustom'd diligence to me.
Now, ye familiar spirits, that are cull'd
Out of the powerful regions under earth,
Help me this once, that France may get the field.

[*They walk, and speak not.*]

O, hold me not with silence over-long!
Where I was wont to feed you with my blood,
I'll lop a member off and give it you,
In earnest of further benefit,
So you do condescend to help me now.

[*They hang their heads.*]

25

No hope to have redress? My body shall
Pay recompense, if you will grant my suit.

[*They shake their heads.*]

Cannot my body nor blood-sacrifice
Entreat you to your wonted furtherance?
Then take my soul; my body, soul and all,
Before that England give the French the foil.

[*They depart.*]

See! They forsake me! Now the time is come
That France must vail her lofty-plumed crest
And let her head fall into England's lap.
My ancient incantations are too weak,
And hell too strong for me to buckle with:
Now, France, thy glory droopeth to the dust.

Suffolk: "I have no power to let her pass" [Act V, Scene 3]

{*The Earl of Suffolk, William de la Pole, has made Margaret of Anjou his prisoner at the battle of Angiers. Though smitten with her, he is married, so he plans to have her marry King Henry VI. (The marriage arrangement he brokers between her father, the King of Naples, and Henry will have dire political repercussions.)*}

I have no power to let her pass;
My hand would free her, but my heart says no
As plays the sun upon the glassy streams,
Twinkling another counterfeited beam,
So seems this gorgeous beauty to mine eyes.
Fain would I woo her, yet I dare not speak:
I'll call for pen and ink, and write my mind.
Fie, de la Pole! Disable not thyself;
Hast not a tongue? Is she not here?
Wilt thou be daunted at a woman's sight?
Ay, beauty's princely majesty is such,
Confounds the tongue and makes the senses rough.

HENRY VI, PART 2

York: "Anjou and Maine are given to the French"
[Act I, Scene 1]

{The Duke of York, Richard Plantagenet, a descendant of Richard II, is furious that King Henry VI has married the relatively impoverished and politically unimportant Margaret of Anjou and given away to her father the lands York himself expected to control in France. York's ultimate ambition, however, is to claim legal title to the crown of England.}

Anjou and Maine are given to the French;
Paris is lost; the state of Normandy
Stands on a tickle point, now they are gone.
Suffolk concluded on the articles,
The peers agreed, and Henry was well pleased
To change two dukedoms for a duke's fair daughter.
I cannot blame them all: what is't to them?
'Tis thine they give away, and not their own.
Pirates may make cheap pennyworths of their pillage
And purchase friends and give to courtesans,
Still revelling like lords till all be gone,
While as the silly owner of the goods
Weeps over them and wrings his hapless hands
And shakes his head and trembling stands aloof,
While all is shared and all is borne away,
Ready to starve and dare not touch his own.
So York must sit and fret and bite his tongue,
While his own lands are bargain'd for and sold.
Methinks the realms of England, France, and Ireland
Bear that proportion to my flesh and blood
As did the fatal brand Althaea burn'd

Unto the prince's heart of Calydon.
Anjou and Maine both given unto the French!
Cold news for me! For I had hope of France,
Even as I have of fertile England's soil.
A day will come when York shall claim his own;
And therefore I will take the Nevils' parts
And make a show of love to proud Duke Humphrey,
And when I spy advantage, claim the crown,
For that's the golden mark I seek to hit.
Nor shall proud Lancaster usurp my right,
Nor hold the sceptre in his childish fist,
Nor wear the diadem upon his head,
Whose church-like humours fits not for a crown.
Then, York, be still awhile, till time do serve.
Watch thou and wake when others be asleep,
To pry into the secrets of the state;
Till Henry, surfeiting in joys of love,
With his new bride and England's dear-bought queen,
And Humphrey with the peers be fall'n at jars:
Then will I raise aloft the milk-white rose,
With whose sweet smell the air shall be perfumed,
And in my standard bear the arms of York
To grapple with the house of Lancaster;
And force perforce, I'll make him yield the crown,
Whose bookish rule hath pull'd fair England down.

Eleanor, Duchess of Gloucester: "Follow I must; I cannot go before" [Act I, Scene 2]

{*Frustrated by the lack of ambition displayed by her husband, Duke Humphrey of Gloucester (the king's uncle), Eleanor must calculate on her own how to bring about King Henry's fall and Gloucester's ascension to the crown.*}

Follow I must; I cannot go before,
While Gloucester bears this base and humble mind.
Were I a man, a duke, and next of blood,
I would remove these tedious stumbling-blocks
And smooth my way upon their headless necks;

And, being a woman, I will not be slack
To play my part in Fortune's pageant.

York: "Now, York, or never, steel thy fearful thoughts"
[Act III, Scene 1]

{*Following a conference with the king, whereby York has helped implicate the king's uncle, the Duke of Gloucester, in a conspiracy against Henry, York is taken out of the picture himself by being sent to quell unrest in Ireland. York sees, however, in this military maneuver an opportunity to launch his own conspiracy against the king in order to lay claim to the throne on the basis of his descent from Richard II.*}

Now, York, or never, steel thy fearful thoughts,
And change misdoubt to resolution.
Be that thou hop'st to be, or what thou art
Resign to death; it is not worth th' enjoying.
Let pale-faced fear keep with the mean-born man,
And find no harbour in a royal heart.
Faster than spring-time show'rs comes thought on thought,
And not a thought but thinks on dignity.
My brain, more busy than the labouring spider,
Weaves tedious snares to trap mine enemies.
Well, nobles, well, 'tis politicly done,
To send me packing with an host of men.
I fear me you but warm the starvèd snake,
Who, cherish'd in your breasts, will sting your hearts.
'Twas men I lack'd and you will give them me;
I take it kindly; and yet be well assured
You put sharp weapons in a madman's hands.
Whiles I in Ireland nourish a mighty band,
I will stir up in England some black storm
Shall blow ten thousand souls to heaven or hell;
And this fell tempest shall not cease to rage
Until the golden circuit on my head,
Like to the glorious sun's transparent beams,
Do calm the fury of this mad-bred flaw.
And, for a minister of my intent,

I have seduced a headstrong Kentishman,
John Cade of Ashford,
To make commotion, as full well he can,
Under the title of John Mortimer.
In Ireland have I seen this stubborn Cade
Oppose himself against a troop of kerns,
And fought so long till that his thighs with darts
Were almost like a sharp-quill'd porpentine;
And, in the end being rescued, I have seen
Him caper upright like a wild Morisco,
Shaking the bloody darts as he his bells.
Full often, like a shag-hair'd crafty kern,
Hath he conversèd with the enemy,
And undiscover'd come to me again
And given me notice of their villainies.
This devil here shall be my substitute;
For that John Mortimer, which now is dead,
In face, in gait, in speech, he doth resemble.
By this I shall perceive the commons' mind,
How they affect the house and claim of York.
Say he be taken, rack'd and torturèd,
I know no pain they can inflict upon him
Will make him say I moved him to those arms.
Say that he thrive, as 'tis great like he will,
Why, then from Ireland come I with my strength
And reap the harvest which that rascal sow'd;
For, Humphrey being dead, as he shall be,
And Henry put apart, the next for me.

King Henry: "O Thou that judgest all things, stay my thoughts" [Act III, Scene 2]

{*In spite of believing in the innocence and good intentions of his uncle, Humphrey, the Duke of Gloucester, King Henry allowed him to be locked up, and now has heard that Gloucester has been murdered "by Suffolk and Cardinal Beaufort's means." King Henry prays before viewing Gloucester's corpse.*}

O Thou that judgest all things, stay my thoughts,
My thoughts that labour to persuade my soul
Some violent hands were laid on Humphrey's life!
If my suspect be false, forgive me, God,
For judgment only doth belong to Thee.
Fain would I go to chafe his paly lips
With twenty thousand kisses, and to drain
Upon his face an ocean of salt tears,
To tell my love unto his dumb deaf trunk,
And with my fingers feel his hand unfeeling.
But all in vain are these mean obsequies;
And to survey his dead and earthy image,
What were it but to make my sorrow greater?

Young Clifford: "Shame and confusion! all is on the rout" [Act V, Scene 2]

{*On the fields of St. Albans, where Lord Thomas Clifford has led a force against the Duke of York's army, "Young" Clifford discovers that his father has been killed by York.*}

Shame and confusion! all is on the rout;
Fear frames disorder, and disorder wounds
Where it should guard. O war, thou son of hell,
Whom angry heavens do make their minister,
Throw in the frozen bosoms of our part
Hot coals of vengeance!—Let no soldier fly:
He that is truly dedicate to war
Hath no self-love; nor he that loves himself

Hath not essentially, but by circumstance,
The name of valour.

[*He sees his dead father.*]

                    O, let the vile world end,
And the premised flames of the last day
Knit earth and heaven together!
Now let the general trumpet blow his blast,
Particularities and petty sounds
To cease!—Wast thou ordain'd, dear father,
To lose thy youth in peace, and to achieve
The silver liv'ry of advisèd age,
And, in thy reverence and thy chair-days, thus
To die in ruffian battle?—Even at this sight
My heart is turn'd to stone: and while 'tis mine,
It shall be stony. York not our old men spares;
No more will I their babes: tears virginal
Shall be to me even as the dew to fire,
And beauty that the tyrant oft reclaims
Shall to my flaming wrath be oil and flax.
Henceforth I will not have to do with pity:
Meet I an infant of the house of York,
Into as many gobbets will I cut it,
As wild Medea young Absyrtus did:
In cruelty will I seek out my fame.
Come, thou new ruin of old Clifford's house:
As did Aeneas old Anchises bear,
So bear I thee upon my manly shoulders;
But then Aeneas bare a living load,
Nothing so heavy as these woes of mine.

HENRY VI, PART 3

Henry: "This battle fares like to the morning's war"
[Act II, Scene 5]

{*During a battle in Yorkshire during England's civil war, King Henry pauses on a hillside to reflect on the destruction before him, where fathers kill sons, sons fathers, and where the Royal forces will lose to the Duke of York's, and he, King Henry himself, will be deposed, captured, and eventually murdered.*}

This battle fares like to the morning's war,
When dying clouds contend with growing light;
What time the shepherd, blowing of his nails,
Can neither call it perfect day nor night.
Now sways it this way, like a mighty sea
Forc'd by the tide to combat with the wind;
Now sways it that way, like the self-same sea
Forced to retire by fury of the wind:
Sometime, the flood prevails, and then, the wind;
Now, one the better; then, another best;
Both tugging to be victors, breast to breast,
Yet neither conqueror nor conquered:
So is the equal poise of this fell war.
Here on this molehill will I sit me down.
To whom God will, there be the victory!
For Margaret my queen, and Clifford too,
Have chid me from the battle, swearing both
They prosper best of all when I am thence.
Would I were dead! if God's good will were so;
For what is in this world but grief and woe?
O God! methinks it were a happy life,
To be no better than a homely swain;
To sit upon a hill, as I do now,
To carve out dials quaintly, point by point,

33

Thereby to see the minutes how they run,
How many make the hour full complete;
How many hours bring about the day;
How many days will finish up the year;
How many years a mortal man may live.
When this is known, then to divide the times:
So many hours must I tend my flock;
So many hours must I take my rest;
So many hours must I contemplate;
So many hours must I sport myself;
So many days my ewes have been with young;
So many weeks ere the poor fools will ean:
So many years ere I shall shear the fleece;
So minutes, hours, days, weeks, months, and years,
Pass'd over to the end they were created,
Would bring white hairs unto a quiet grave.
Ah, what a life were this! how sweet! how lovely!
Gives not the hawthorn-bush a sweeter shade
To shepherds looking on their silly sheep,
Than doth a rich embroider'd canopy
To kings that fear their subjects' treachery?
O, yes, it doth; a thousand-fold it doth.
And to conclude, the shepherd's homely curds,
His cold thin drink out of his leather bottle,
His wonted sleep under a fresh tree's shade,
All which secure and sweetly he enjoys,
Is far beyond a prince's delicates,
His viands sparkling in a golden cup,
His body couchèd in a curious bed,
When care, mistrust, and treason waits on him.

Clifford: "Here burns my candle out; ay, here it dies"
[Act II, Scene 6]

{*Wounded on a field of battle at Ferrybridge in Yorkshire, Lord John Clifford (formerly "Young" Clifford) sees his end. The Duke of York has defeated the Royal army that Clifford has led for Queen Margaret.*}

Here burns my candle out; ay, here it dies,
Which, whiles it lasted, gave King Henry light.
O Lancaster, I fear thy overthrow
More than my body's parting with my soul!
My love and fear glued many friends to thee;
And, now I fall, thy tough commixture melts.
Impairing Henry, strengthening misproud York,
The common people swarm like summer flies:
And whither fly the gnats but to the sun?
And who shines now but Henry's enemies?
O Phoebus, hadst thou never given consent
That Phaethon should check thy fiery steeds,
Thy burning car never had scorch'd the earth!
And, Henry, hadst thou sway'd as kings should do,
Or as thy father and his father did,
Giving no ground unto the house of York,
They never then had sprung like summer flies;
I and ten thousand in this luckless realm
Had left no mourning widows for our death;
And thou this day hadst kept thy chair in peace.
For what doth cherish weeds but gentle air?
And what makes robbers bold but too much lenity?
Bootless are plaints, and cureless are my wounds;
No way to fly, nor strength to hold out flight:
The foe is merciless, and will not pity;
For, at their hands, I have deserved no pity.
The air hath got into my deadly wounds,
And much effuse of blood doth make me faint:
Come, York, and Richard, Warwick, and the rest;
I stabb'd your fathers' bosoms, split my breast.

[*He faints.*]

Richard, Duke of Gloucester: "Ay, Edward will use women honourably" [Act III, Scene 2]

{*Upon the capture of Henry VI in the Wars of the Roses, Edward IV has assumed the throne of England. Meanwhile, in London, at the royal palace, his younger brother Richard, Duke of Gloucester, continues his scheme to do away with the human impediments to his own ascension to the kingship.*}

Ay, Edward will use women honourably.
Would he were wasted, marrow, bones, and all,
That from his loins no hopeful branch may spring,
To cross me from the golden time I look for!
And yet, between my soul's desire and me—
The lustful Edward's title buried—
Is Clarence, Henry, and his son young Edward,
And all the unlook'd for issue of their bodies,
To take their rooms, ere I can place myself:
A cold premeditation for my purpose!
Why, then, I do but dream on sovereignty;
Like one that stands upon a promontory,
And spies a far-off shore where he would tread,
Wishing his foot were equal with his eye,
And chides the sea that sunders him from thence,
Saying, he'll lade it dry to have his way:
So do I wish the crown, being so far off;
And so I chide the means that keeps me from it;
And so I say, I'll cut the causes off,
Flattering me with impossibilities.
My eye's too quick, my heart o'erweens too much,
Unless my hand and strength could equal them.
Well, say there is no kingdom then for Richard;
What other pleasure can the world afford?
I'll make my heaven in a lady's lap,
And deck my body in gay ornaments,
And witch sweet ladies with my words and looks.
O miserable thought! and more unlikely
Than to accomplish twenty golden crowns!
Why, love forswore me in my mother's womb:
And, for I should not deal in her soft laws,
She did corrupt frail nature with some bribe,

To shrink mine arm up like a wither'd shrub;
To make an envious mountain on my back,
Where sits deformity to mock my body;
To shape my legs of an unequal size;
To disproportion me in every part,
Like to a chaos, or an unlick'd bear-whelp
That carries no impression like the dam.
And am I then a man to be belov'd?
O monstrous fault, to harbour such a thought!
Then, since this earth affords no joy to me,
But to command, to check, to o'erbear such
As are of better person than myself,
I'll make my heaven to dream upon the crown,
And, whiles I live, to account this world but hell,
Until my mis-shap'd trunk that bears this head
Be round impaled with a glorious crown.
And yet I know not how to get the crown,
For many lives stand between me and home:
And I—like one lost in a thorny wood,
That rends the thorns and is rent with the thorns,
Seeking a way and straying from the way;
Not knowing how to find the open air,
But toiling desperately to find it out—
Torment myself to catch the English crown:
And from that torment I will free myself,
Or hew my way out with a bloody axe.
Why, I can smile and murder whiles I smile,
And cry "Content" to that which grieves my heart,
And wet my cheeks with artificial tears,
And frame my face to all occasions.
I'll drown more sailors than the mermaid shall;
I'll slay more gazers than the basilisk;
I'll play the orator as well as Nestor,
Deceive more slily than Ulysses could,
And, like a Sinon, take another Troy:
I can add colours to the chameleon,
Change shapes with Proteus for advantages,
And set the murderous Machiavel to school.
Can I do this, and cannot get a crown?
Tut! were it farther off, I'll pluck it down.

Warwick: "Ah, who is nigh? Come to me, friend or foe"
[Act V, Scene 2]

{*The Earl of Warwick has been left for dead by Edward IV at the battle of Barnet. Formerly his ally, Warwick turned against Edward and the "Yorkists" during Edward's invasion from France.*}

Ah, who is nigh? Come to me, friend or foe,
And tell me, who is victor, York or Warwick?
Why ask I that? My mangled body shows,
My blood, my want of strength, my sick heart shows,
That I must yield my body to the earth,
And, by my fall, the conquest to my foe.
Thus yields the cedar to the axe's edge,
Whose arms gave shelter to the princely eagle,
Under whose shade the ramping lion slept,
Whose top-branch overpeer'd Jove's spreading tree
And kept low shrubs from winter's powerful wind.
These eyes, that now are dimm'd with death's black veil,
Have been as piercing as the mid-day sun,
To search the secret treasons of the world:
The wrinkles in my brows, now filled with blood,
Were liken'd oft to kingly sepulchres;
For who liv'd king, but I could dig his grave?
And who durst smile when Warwick bent his brow?
Lo, now my glory smear'd in dust and blood!
My parks, my walks, my manors that I had,
Even now forsake me, and of all my lands,
Is nothing left me but my body's length.
Why, what is pomp, rule, reign, but earth and dust?
And, live we how we can, yet die we must.

Richard, Duke of Gloucester: "What, will the aspiring blood of Lancaster" [Act V, Scene 6]

{*The Duke of Gloucester has assassinated the peaceful Christian King Henry VI in the Tower of London, thus clearing one hurdle on his path to the throne.*}

What, will the aspiring blood of Lancaster
Sink in the ground? I thought it would have mounted.
See, how my sword weeps for the poor king's death!
O, may such purple tears be always shed
From those that wish the downfall of our house!
If any spark of life be yet remaining,
Down, down to hell; and say I sent thee thither:

[*Richard again stabs the already dead Henry VI.*]

I, that have neither pity, love, nor fear.
Indeed, 'tis true that Henry told me of;
For I have often heard my mother say
I came into the world with my legs forward:
Had I not reason, think ye, to make haste,
And seek their ruin that usurp'd our right?
The midwife wonder'd and the women cried,
"O, Jesus, bless us, he is born with teeth!"
And so I was; which plainly signified
That I should snarl and bite and play the dog.
Then, since the heavens have shap'd my body so,
Let hell make crook'd my mind to answer it.
I have no brother, I am like no brother;
And this word "love," which graybeards call divine,
Be resident in men like one another
And not in me: I am myself alone.
Clarence, beware; thou keep'st me from the light:
But I will sort a pitchy day for thee;
For I will buzz abroad such prophecies
That Edward shall be fearful of his life,
And then, to purge his fear, I'll be thy death.
King Henry and the prince his son are gone:
Clarence, thy turn is next, and then the rest;
Counting myself but bad till I be best.
I'll throw thy body in another room
And triumph, Henry, in thy day of doom.

HENRY VIII

Cardinal Wolsey: "So farewell to the little good you bear me" [Act III, Scene 2]

{*Cardinal Wolsey sees no way out of the catastrophe he has created himself. Once a powerful man in Henry VIII's government, he has made enemies through his destruction of the Duke of Buckingham; now the king has been shown papers detailing Wolsey's ill-gotten financial gains as well as letters to the Pope arguing against Henry's desired divorce.*}

So farewell to the little good you bear me.
Farewell! a long farewell to all my greatness!
This is the state of man: today he puts forth
The tender leaves of hopes; tomorrow blossoms,
And bears his blushing honours thick upon him;
The third day comes a frost, a killing frost,
And, when he thinks, good easy man, full surely
His greatness is a-ripening, nips his root,
And then he falls, as I do. I have ventured,
Like little wanton boys that swim on bladders,
This many summers in a sea of glory,
But far beyond my depth. My high-blown pride
At length broke under me and now has left me,
Weary and old with service, to the mercy
Of a rude stream that must for ever hide me.
Vain pomp and glory of this world, I hate ye!
I feel my heart new open'd. O, how wretched
Is that poor man that hangs on princes' favours!
There is, betwixt that smile we would aspire to,
That sweet aspect of princes, and their ruin,
More pangs and fears than wars or women have:
And when he falls, he falls like Lucifer,
Never to hope again.

JULIUS CAESAR

Brutus: "Since Cassius first did whet me against Caesar"
[Act II, Scene 1]

{*In the middle of the night, on the eve of the fateful Ides of March, Brutus, Julius Caesar's friend, is awake, troubled by his having been persuaded by Caesar's enemies that Caesar's aspirations to become emperor of Rome will be the Roman republic's downfall, and that Caesar must be assassinated.*}

Since Cassius first did whet me against Caesar,
I have not slept.
Between the acting of a dreadful thing
And the first motion, all the interim is
Like a phantasma, or a hideous dream:
The genius and the mortal instruments
Are then in council; and the state of man,
Like to a little kingdom, suffers then
The nature of an insurrection.

Brutus: "O conspiracy!/Sham'st thou to show thy
dangerous brow by night" [Act II, Scene 1]

{*As in the previous soliloquy, given moments before, Brutus continues contemplating the fatal action he has agreed to take against Caesar.*}

                              O conspiracy!
Sham'st thou to show thy dangerous brow by night,
When evils are most free? O, then by day
Where wilt thou find a cavern dark enough
To mask thy monstrous visage? Seek none, conspiracy;
Hide it in smiles and affability:

For if thou path, thy native semblance on,
Not Erebus itself were dim enough
To hide thee from prevention.

Antony: "O, pardon me, thou bleeding piece of earth"
[Act III, Scene 1]

{*At the Roman capitol, Antony, who promoted Julius Caesar's being named emperor, has just met with Caesar's assassins, with whom he has pretended to sympathize. He apologizes to the corpse of his friend as he prepares himself for revenge.*}

O, pardon me, thou bleeding piece of earth,
That I am meek and gentle with these butchers!
Thou art the ruins of the noblest man
That ever lived in the tide of times.
Woe to the hand that shed this costly blood!
Over thy wounds now do I prophesy,
Which like dumb mouths do ope their ruby lips,
To beg the voice and utterance of my tongue,
A curse shall light upon the limbs of men;
Domestic fury and fierce civil strife
Shall cumber all the parts of Italy;
Blood and destruction shall be so in use,
And dreadful objects so familiar,
That mothers shall but smile when they behold
Their infants quarter'd with the hands of war;
All pity chok'd with custom of fell deeds:
And Caesar's spirit, ranging for revenge,
With Àte by his side come hot from hell,
Shall in these confines with a monarch's voice
Cry, "Havoc!" and let slip the dogs of war;
That this foul deed shall smell above the earth
With carrion men, groaning for burial.

KING JOHN

Philip the Bastard: "Mad world! Mad kings! Mad composition!" [Act II, Scene 1]

{*Philip Faulconbridge, the bastard son of the former king, Richard the Lion-Hearted, comments on the politics of the complex treaty between England's King John and France's King Philip and muses on his own cunning strategies for the future.*}

Mad world! Mad kings! Mad composition!
John, to stop Arthur's title in the whole,
Hath willingly departed with a part,
And France, whose armour conscience buckled on,
Whom zeal and charity brought to the field
As God's own soldier, rounded in the ear
With that same purpose-changer, that sly devil,
That broker, that still breaks the pate of faith,
That daily break-vow, he that wins of all,
Of kings, of beggars, old men, young men, maids,
Who, having no external thing to lose
But the word "maid," cheats the poor maid of that,
That smooth-faced gentleman, tickling commodity,
Commodity, the bias of the world,
The world who of itself is peiséd well,
Made to run even upon even ground,
Till this advantage, this vile-drawing bias,
This sway of motion, this commodity,
Makes it take head from all indifferency,
From all direction, purpose, course, intent:
And this same bias, this commodity,
This bawd, this broker, this all-changing word,
Clapp'd on the outward eye of fickle France,

Hath drawn him from his own determined aid,
From a resolved and honourable war,
To a most base and vile-concluded peace.
And why rail I on this commodity?
But for because he hath not woo'd me yet:
Not that I have the power to clutch my hand,
When his fair angels would salute my palm;
But for my hand, as unattempted yet,
Like a poor beggar, raileth on the rich.
Well, whiles I am a beggar, I will rail
And say there is no sin but to be rich;
And being rich, my virtue then shall be
To say there is no vice but beggary.
Since kings break faith upon commodity,
Gain, be my lord, for I will worship thee!

KING LEAR

Edmund: "Thou, Nature, art my goddess; to thy law"
[Act I, Scene 2]

{*In a hall in his father the Earl of Gloucester's castle, Edmund, a forged letter in hand, begins his machinations to destroy his older (and legitimate) brother Edgar's inheritance of the earldom.*}

Thou, Nature, art my goddess; to thy law
My services are bound. Wherefore should I
Stand in the plague of custom, and permit
The curiosity of nations to deprive me,
For that I am some twelve or fourteen moonshines
Lag of a brother? Why bastard? wherefore base?
When my dimensions are as well compact,
My mind as generous, and my shape as true,
As honest madam's issue? Why brand they us
With base? with baseness? bastardy? base, base?
Who in the lusty stealth of nature take
More composition and fierce quality
Than doth, within a dull, stale, tired bed,
Go to the creating a whole tribe of fops,
Got 'tween asleep and wake? Well, then,
Legitimate Edgar, I must have your land:
Our father's love is to the bastard Edmund
As to the legitimate: fine word, "legitimate"!
Well, my legitimate, if this letter speed,
And my invention thrive, Edmund the base
Shall top the legitimate.—I grow, I prosper;
Now, gods, stand up for bastards!

Edmund: "This is the excellent foppery of the world, that, when we are sick in fortune . . ." [Act I, Scene 2]

{*By means of a forged letter implicating Edgar in a murder conspiracy against Gloucester, Edmund, the Earl of Gloucester's bastard, has turned his father against Edgar, the legitimate heir. The Earl has ranted about Edgar's supposed villainy, blaming, among other factors, the astrological conditions.*}

This is the excellent foppery of the world, that, when we are sick in fortune—often the surfeit of our own behavior—we make guilty of our disasters the sun, the moon, and the stars; as if we were villains by necessity, fools by heavenly compulsion, knaves, thieves, and treachers by spherical predominance; drunkards, liars, and adulterers by an enforced obedience of planetary influence; and all that we are evil in, by a divine thrusting on: an admirable evasion of whoremaster man, to lay his goatish disposition to the charge of a star! My father compounded with my mother under the dragon's tail, and my nativity was under Ursa major; so that it follows I am rough and lecherous. 'Sfoot! I should have been that I am had the maidenliest star in the firmament twinkled on my bastardizing.

Lear: "Blow, winds, and crack your cheeks! rage! blow!" [Act III, Scene 2]

{*Out on the heath in Gloucestershire, amid a storm, King Lear is accompanied by his fool but seemingly unaware of him and his remarks. The maddened king, disposed of and betrayed by two of his daughters, calls down more suffering.*}

Blow, winds, and crack your cheeks! rage! blow!
You cataracts and hurricanoes, spout
Till you have drench'd our steeples, drown'd the cocks!
You sulphurous and thought-executing fires,
Vaunt-couriers to oak-cleaving thunderbolts,
Singe my white head! And thou, all-shaking thunder,
Strike flat the thick rotundity o' the world!
Crack nature's moulds, all germens spill at once
That make ingrateful man!

Rumble thy bellyful! Spit, fire! spout, rain!
Nor rain, wind, thunder, fire, are my daughters:
I tax not you, you elements, with unkindness;
I never gave you kingdom, call'd you children,
You owe me no subscription: then let fall
Your horrible pleasure; here I stand, your slave,
A poor, infirm, weak, and despisèd old man.
But yet I call you servile ministers,
That have with two pernicious daughters join'd
Your high-engender'd battles 'gainst a head
So old and white as this. O! O! 'tis foul!

Edgar: "When we our betters see bearing our woes" [Act III, Scene 6]

{*Edgar, having fled from his father's mistaken wrath, has been disguised as a beggar while helping poor old mad Lear. After here reflecting on his own suffering compared to that of Lear's, Edgar will take revenge on his villainous brother Edmund.*}

When we our betters see bearing our woes,
We scarcely think our miseries our foes.
Who alone suffers suffers most i' the mind,
Leaving free things and happy shows behind;
But then the mind much sufferance doth o'er skip,
When grief hath mates, and bearing fellowship.
How light and portable my pain seems now,
When that which makes me bend makes the king bow;
He childed as I father'd! Tom, away!
Mark the high noises, and thyself bewray,
When false opinion, whose wrong thought defiles thee,
In thy just proof, repeals and reconciles thee.
What will hap more tonight, safe 'scape the king!
Lurk, lurk.

LOVE'S LABOUR'S LOST

Armado: "I do affect the very ground, which is base, where her shoe, which is baser, guided by her foot, which is basest, doth tread." [Act I, Scene 2]

{*The braggart Don Adriano de Armado, "a fantastical Spaniard," is in love with Jacquenetta, a young woman far beneath him in social status, but pour his heart out he must.*}

I do affect the very ground, which is base, where her shoe, which is baser, guided by her foot, which is basest, doth tread. I shall be forsworn, which is a great argument of falsehood, if I love. And how can that be true love which is falsely attempted? Love is a familiar; Love is a devil: there is no evil angel but Love. Yet was Samson so tempted, and he had an excellent strength; yet was Solomon so seduced, and he had a very good wit. Cupid's butt-shaft is too hard for Hercules' club, and therefore too much odds for a Spaniard's rapier. The first and second cause will not serve my turn; the passado he respects not, the duello he regards not: his disgrace is to be called boy; but his glory is to subdue men. Adieu, valour! Rust, rapier! Be still, drum! For your manager is in love; yea, he loveth. Assist me, some extemporal god of rhyme, for I am sure I shall turn sonnet. Devise, wit! Write, pen! For I am for whole volumes in folio.

Berowne: "And I, forsooth, in love!" [Act III, Scene 1]

{*As one of the lords who has agreed with the King of Navarre's edict against love, so that the young men's minds would be better focused on studying, Berowne finds himself madly in love with Rosaline, to whom he has written declaring his love.*}

And I, forsooth, in love!
I, that have been love's whip,
A very beadle to a humorous sigh;
A critic, nay, a night-watch constable,
A domineering pedant o'er the boy,
Than whom no mortal so magnificent!
This whimpled, whining, purblind, wayward boy,
This Signor Junior, giant-dwarf, Dan Cupid,
Regent of love-rhymes, lord of folded arms,
The anointed sovereign of sighs and groans,
Liege of all loiterers and malcontents,
Dread prince of plackets, king of codpieces,
Sole imperator and great general
Of trotting paritors.—O my little heart!
And I to be a corporal of his field,
And wear his colours like a tumbler's hoop!
What? I love! I sue! I seek a wife!
A woman, that is like a German clock,
Still a-repairing, ever out of frame,
And never going aright, being a watch,
But being watch'd that it may still go right!
Nay, to be perjured, which is worst of all;
And, among three, to love the worst of all;
A whitely wanton with a velvet brow,
With two pitch-balls stuck in her face for eyes;
Ay, and by heaven, one that will do the deed
Though Argus were her eunuch and her guard:
And I to sigh for her! to watch for her!
To pray for her! Go to; it is a plague
That Cupid will impose for my neglect
Of his almighty dreadful little might.
Well, I will love, write, sigh, pray, sue and groan:
Some men must love my lady and some Joan.

MACBETH

Macbeth: "This supernatural soliciting/Cannot be ill, cannot be good . . ." [Act I, Scene 3]

{*Macbeth, a general of the King of Scotland's army, has visited with his co-general Banquo and three witches, "the weird sisters," who foretell that Macbeth will become king. While he contemplates this prediction, Banquo consults with two noblemen, and they remark on Macbeth's preoccupation.*}

This supernatural soliciting
Cannot be ill, cannot be good: if ill,
Why hath it given me earnest of success,
Commencing in a truth? I am thane of Cawdor:
If good, why do I yield to that suggestion
Whose horrid image doth unfix my hair
And make my seated heart knock at my ribs,
Against the use of nature? Present fears
Are less than horrible imaginings:
My thought, whose murder yet is but fantastical,
Shakes so my single state of man that function
Is smother'd in surmise, and nothing is
But what is not.

If chance will have me king, why, chance may crown me,
Without my stir.

Come what come may,
Time and the hour runs through the longest day.

Lady Macbeth: "They met me in the day of success; and I have learned by the perfectest report, they have more in them than mortal knowledge." [Act I, Scene 5]

{Lady Macbeth enters reading the letter that she has received from her husband. It details the visit he made with Banquo to the witches. More ambitious, less scrupulous than Macbeth, she ponders his character.}

"They met me in the day of success; and I have learned by the perfectest report, they have more in them than mortal knowledge. When I burned in desire to question them further, they made themselves air, into which they vanished. Whiles I stood rapt in the wonder of it, came missives from the king, who all-hailed me 'Thane of Cawdor,' by which title, before, these weird sisters saluted me, and referred me to the coming on of time, with 'Hail, king that shalt be!' This have I thought good to deliver thee, my dearest partner of greatness, that thou mightst not lose the dues of rejoicing, by being ignorant of what greatness is promised thee. Lay it to thy heart, and farewell."

Glamis thou art, and Cawdor; and shalt be
What thou art promised: yet do I fear thy nature;
It is too full o' the milk of human kindness
To catch the nearest way: thou wouldst be great;
Art not without ambition, but without
The illness should attend it: what thou wouldst highly,
That wouldst thou holily; wouldst not play false,
And yet wouldst wrongly win: thou'ldst have, great Glamis,
That which cries, "Thus thou must do, if thou have it;
And that which rather thou dost fear to do
Than wishest should be undone." Hie thee hither,
That I may pour my spirits in thine ear,
And chastise with the valour of my tongue
All that impedes thee from the golden round,
Which fate and metaphysical aid doth seem
To have thee crown'd withal.

Lady Macbeth: "The raven himself is hoarse"
[Act I, Scene 5]

{Moments after musing on her husband's news (see previous soliloquy), Lady Macbeth hears word of the arrival at her castle of Duncan, the King of Scotland.}

The raven himself is hoarse
That croaks the fatal entrance of Duncan
Under my battlements. Come, you spirits
That tend on mortal thoughts, unsex me here,
And fill me, from the crown to the toe, top-full
Of direst cruelty! Make thick my blood,
Stop up the access and passage to remorse,
That no compunctious visitings of nature
Shake my fell purpose, nor keep peace between
The effect and it! Come to my woman's breasts,
And take my milk for gall, you murdering ministers,
Wherever in your sightless substances
You wait on nature's mischief! Come, thick night,
And pall thee in the dunnest smoke of hell,
That my keen knife see not the wound it makes,
Nor heaven peep through the blanket of the dark,
To cry "Hold, hold!"

Macbeth: "Is this a dagger which I see before me"
[Act II, Scene 1]

{Macbeth prepares to sneak into the king's room and murder him with the weapon Lady Macbeth has provided.}

Is this a dagger which I see before me,
The handle toward my hand? Come, let me clutch thee.
I have thee not, and yet I see thee still.
Art thou not, fatal vision, sensible
To feeling as to sight? Or art thou but
A dagger of the mind, a false creation,
Proceeding from the heat-oppressed brain?
I see thee yet, in form as palpable

As this which now I draw.
Thou marshall'st me the way that I was going;
And such an instrument I was to use.
Mine eyes are made the fools o' the other senses,
Or else worth all the rest: I see thee still;
And on thy blade and dudgeon gouts of blood,
Which was not so before. There's no such thing:
It is the bloody business which informs
Thus to mine eyes. Now o'er the one half-world
Nature seems dead, and wicked dreams abuse
The curtain'd sleep; witchcraft celebrates
Pale Hecate's offerings; and wither'd murder,
Alarum'd by his sentinel, the wolf,
Whose howl's his watch, thus with his stealthy pace,
With Tarquin's ravishing strides, towards his design
Moves like a ghost. Thou sure and firm-set earth,
Hear not my steps, which way they walk, for fear
Thy very stones prate of my whereabout,
And take the present horror from the time,
Which now suits with it. Whiles I threat, he lives:
Words to the heat of deeds too cold breath gives.

[*A bell rings.*]

I go, and it is done: the bell invites me.
Hear it not, Duncan; for it is a knell
That summons thee to heaven, or to hell.

Porter: "Here's a knocking indeed!" [Act II, Scene 3]

{*On the night of the as yet unrevealed murder of Duncan, the Macbeths' porter goes to answer the knocking at the gate. He will let in Macduff and Lennox, who eventually unravel and avenge the murder.*}

[*Knocking within.*]

Here's a knocking indeed! If a man were porter of hell-gate, he should have old turning the key.

[*Knocking within.*]

Knock, knock, knock! Who's there, i' the name of Beelzebub? Here's a farmer, that hanged himself on the expectation of plenty: come in time; have napkins enow about you; here you'll sweat for't.

[*Knocking within.*]

Knock, knock! Who's there, in th' other devil's name? Faith, here's an equivocator, that could swear in both the scales against either scale; who committed treason enough for God's sake, yet could not equivocate to heaven: O, come in, equivocator.

[*Knocking within.*]

Knock, knock, knock! Who's there? Faith, here's an English tailor come hither, for stealing out of a French hose. Come in, tailor; here you may roast your goose.

[*Knocking within.*]

Knock, knock; never at quiet! What are you? But this place is too cold for hell. I'll devil-porter it no further: I had thought to have let in some of all professions that go the primrose way to the everlasting bonfire.

[*Knocking within.*]

Anon, anon! I pray you, remember the porter.

Lady Macbeth: "Yet here's a spot" [Act V, Scene 1]

{*Though having obtained her wish of becoming queen, guilt-ridden Lady Macbeth is observed sleepwalking by a doctor and waiting-woman, who comment on her tormented and telling mutterings. "Her eyes are open," remarks the doctor; "but their sense is shut," explains the waiting-woman. "Look, how she rubs her hands," notes the doctor. "It is an accustomed action with her," says the waiting-woman. The [. . .] in the text indicates an observation by the doctor or waiting-woman.*}

Yet here's a spot.

[. . .]

Out, damned spot! out, I say! One: two: why, then, 'tis time to do't. Hell is murky! Fie, my lord, fie! a soldier, and afeard? What need we fear who knows it, when none can call our power to account? Yet who would have thought the old man to have had so much blood in him?

[...]

The thane of Fife had a wife: where is she now? What, will these hands ne'er be clean? No more o' that, my lord, no more o' that: you mar all with this starting.

[...]

Here's the smell of the blood still: all the perfumes of Arabia will not sweeten this little hand. Oh, oh, oh!

[...]

Wash your hands; put on your nightgown; look not so pale: I tell you yet again, Banquo's buried; he cannot come out on's grave.

[...]

To bed, to bed! there's knocking at the gate: come, come, come, come, give me your hand: what's done cannot be undone. To bed, to bed, to bed!

MEASURE FOR MEASURE

Angelo: "What's this? What's this? Is this her fault or mine?"
[Act II, Scene 2]

{*Angelo, deputized by the Duke of Vienna to enforce "morality" laws, has sentenced a young man to death for getting his fiancée pregnant. The young man's sister, Isabella, a novice nun, has gone to Angelo to plead for mercy. Angelo discovers that in spite of himself he is enraptured.*}

What's this? What's this? Is this her fault or mine?
The tempter or the tempted, who sins most?
Ha!
Not she: nor doth she tempt: but it is I
That, lying by the violet in the sun,
Do as the carrion does, not as the flower,
Corrupt with virtuous season. Can it be
That modesty may more betray our sense
Than woman's lightness? Having waste ground enough,
Shall we desire to raze the sanctuary
And pitch our evils there? O, fie, fie, fie!
What dost thou, or what art thou, Angelo?
Dost thou desire her foully for those things
That make her good? O, let her brother live!
Thieves for their robbery have authority
When judges steal themselves. What, do I love her,
That I desire to hear her speak again,
And feast upon her eyes? What is't I dream on?
O cunning enemy that to catch a saint,
With saints dost bait thy hook! Most dangerous
Is that temptation that doth goad us on
To sin in loving virtue. Never could the strumpet,
With all her double vigour, art and nature,

Once stir my temper; but this virtuous maid
Subdues me quite. Even till now,
When men were fond, I smiled and wonder'd how.

Angelo: "When I would pray and think, I think and pray" [Act II, Scene 4]

{Angelo, unable to free himself of Isabella's image, contemplates his dilemma. Proud of his inflexibility about enforcing morality laws, he nevertheless finds himself tempted to exploit his power over Isabella.}

When I would pray and think, I think and pray
To several subjects. Heaven hath my empty words,
Whilst my invention, hearing not my tongue,
Anchors on Isabel: Heaven in my mouth,
As if I did but only chew his name;
And in my heart the strong and swelling evil
Of my conception. The state, whereon I studied,
Is like a good thing, being often read,
Grown fear'd and tedious; yea, my gravity,
Wherein—let no man hear me—I take pride,
Could I, with boot, change for an idle plume,
Which the air beats for vain. O place, O form,
How often dost thou with thy case, thy habit,
Wrench awe from fools and tie the wiser souls
To thy false seeming! Blood, thou art blood:
Let's write "Good Angel" on the devil's horn:
'Tis not the devil's crest.

Isabella: "To whom should I complain? Did I tell this"
[Act II, Scene 4]

{The pious novice Isabella is staggered hearing Angelo's proposal: her virginity sacrificed to him in exchange for her brother's life.}

To whom should I complain? Did I tell this,
Who would believe me? O perilous mouths,
That bear in them one and the self-same tongue,
Either of condemnation or approof;
Bidding the law make court'sy to their will:
Hooking both right and wrong to th' appetite,
To follow as it draws! I'll to my brother:
Though he hath fallen by prompture of the blood,
Yet hath he in him such a mind of honour
That, had he twenty heads to tender down
On twenty bloody blocks, he'ld yield them up,
Before his sister should her body stoop
To such abhorr'd pollution.
Then, Isabel, live chaste, and, brother, die:
More than our brother is our chastity.
I'll tell him yet of Angelo's request,
And fit his mind to death, for his soul's rest.

Duke: "He who the sword of heaven will bear"
[Act III, Scene 2]

{Vincentio, the Duke of Vienna, who has left Angelo to rule and to enforce disregarded laws, now condemns his deputy for being too zealous in his application of the laws. He outlines his plans to expose Angelo's hypocrisy by tricking Angelo into sleeping not with the innocent Isabella but with his betrayed fianceé.}

He who the sword of heaven will bear
Should be as holy as severe;
Pattern in himself to know,
Grace to stand, and virtue go;
More nor less to others paying
Than by self-offences weighing.
Shame to him whose cruel striking

Kills for faults of his own liking!
Twice treble shame on Angelo,
To weed my vice and let his grow!
O, what may man within him hide,
Though angel on the outward side!
How may likeness made in crimes,
Making practice on the times,
To draw with idle spiders' strings
Most ponderous and substantial things!
Craft against vice I must apply;
With Angelo tonight shall lie
His old betrothèd but despisèd;
So disguise shall, by the disguisèd,
Pay with falsehood false exacting,
And perform an old contracting.

Angelo: "This deed unshapes me quite, makes me unpregnant" [Act IV, Scene 4]

{*Angelo rues the contemptible acts that he believes he has committed: sleeping with Isabella in exchange for freeing her brother but then having him executed. The woman he has slept with is, rather, his former fianceé Mariana in Isabella's place; Claudio, Isabella's brother, has not been executed, in spite of the orders.*}

This deed unshapes me quite, makes me unpregnant
And dull to all proceedings. A deflower'd maid!
And by an eminent body that enforced
The law against it! But that her tender shame
Will not proclaim against her maiden loss,
How might she tongue me! Yet reason dares her no;
For my authority bears of a credent bulk,
That no particular scandal once can touch
But it confounds the breather. He should have lived,
Save that this riotous youth, with dangerous sense,
Might in the times to come have ta'en revenge,
By so receiving a dishonour'd life
With ransom of such shame. Would yet he had lived!
Alack, when once our grace we have forgot,
Nothing goes right: we would, and we would not.

THE MERRY WIVES OF WINDSOR

Ford: "What a damned Epicurean rascal is this!"
[Act II, Scene 2]

{*Master Ford, a gentleman of Windsor, suspecting his wife of betraying him, has disguised himself as a "Master Brook" to inveigle the rogue Sir John Falstaff into discovering his wife's infidelity, but learns that she has already made an appointment to be with Falstaff that night. Ford is unaware that she and her friend Mistress Page are leading on Falstaff to punish him for his audacity.*}

What a damned Epicurean rascal is this! My heart is ready to crack with impatience. Who says this is improvident jealousy? My wife hath sent to him; the hour is fixed; the match is made. Would any man have thought this? See the hell of having a false woman! My bed shall be abused, my coffers ransacked, my reputation gnawn at; and I shall not only receive this villainous wrong, but stand under the adoption of abominable terms, and by him that does me this wrong. Terms! names! Amaimon sounds well; Lucifer, well; Barbason, well; yet they are devils' additions, the names of fiends. But cuckold! Wittol!—Cuckold! The devil himself hath not such a name. Page is an ass, a secure ass. He will trust his wife; he will not be jealous. I will rather trust a Fleming with my butter, Parson Hugh the Welshman with my cheese, an Irishman with my aqua-vitae bottle, or a thief to walk my ambling gelding, than my wife with herself. Then she plots, then she ruminates, then she devises; and what they think in their hearts they may effect, they will break their hearts but they will effect. God be praised for my jealousy! Eleven o'clock the hour. I will prevent this, detect my wife, be revenged on Falstaff, and laugh at Page. I will about it; better three hours too soon than a minute too late. Fie, fie, fie! Cuckold! cuckold! cuckold!

Falstaff: "The Windsor bell hath struck twelve; the minute draws on." [Act V, Scene 5]

{Wearing a buck's head, as requested by some merry wives, Falstaff readies himself for a night of debauchery in the forest. Little does he know that he is the subject of an elaborate scheme to expose him.}

The Windsor bell hath struck twelve; the minute draws on. Now, the hot-blooded gods assist me! Remember, Jove, thou wast a bull for thy Europa; love set on thy horns. O powerful Love, that in some respects makes a beast a man, in some other, a man a beast. You were also, Jupiter, a swan for the love of Leda. O omnipotent Love! how near the god drew to the complexion of a goose! A fault done first in the form of a beast. O Jove, a beastly fault! And then another fault in the semblance of a fowl. Think on't, Jove; a foul fault! When gods have hot backs, what shall poor men do? For me, I am here a Windsor stag; and the fattest, I think, i' the forest. Send me a cool rut-time, Jove, or who can blame me to piss my tallow? Who comes here? My doe?

A MIDSUMMER NIGHT'S DREAM

Helena: "How happy some o'er other some can be!"
[Act I, Scene 1]

{*Helena, a young woman, loves Demetrius, but he is in love with her friend Hermia. Hermia and Lysander, meanwhile, have told her of their plans to elope. Helena contemplates the nature of love.*}

How happy some o'er other some can be!
Through Athens I am thought as fair as she.
But what of that? Demetrius thinks not so;
He will not know what all but he do know:
And as he errs, doting on Hermia's eyes,
So I, admiring of his qualities:
Things base and vile, holding no quantity,
Love can transpose to form and dignity.
Love looks not with the eyes, but with the mind;
And therefore is wing'd Cupid painted blind:
Nor hath Love's mind of any judgement taste;
Wings and no eyes figure unheedy haste:
And therefore is Love said to be a child,
Because in choice he is so oft beguiled.
As waggish boys in game themselves forswear,
So the boy Love is perjured everywhere:
For ere Demetrius look'd on Hermia's eyne,
He hail'd down oaths that he was only mine;
And when this hail some heat from Hermia felt,
So he dissolved, and showers of oaths did melt.
I will go tell him of fair Hermia's flight:
Then to the wood will he tomorrow night
Pursue her; and for this intelligence

If I have thanks, it is a dear expense:
But herein mean I to enrich my pain,
To have his sight thither and back again.

Helena: "O, I am out of breath in this fond chase"
[Act II, Scene 2]

{*After Demetrius (chased by Helena) exits, Helena, out of breath, bemoans her state and compares her looks to Hermia's.*}

O, I am out of breath in this fond chase.
The more my prayer, the lesser is my grace.
Happy is Hermia, wheresoe'er she lies,
For she hath blessèd and attractive eyes.
How came her eyes so bright? Not with salt tears:
If so, my eyes are oft'ner wash'd than hers.
No, no! I am as ugly as a bear;
For beasts that meet me run away for fear.
Therefore no marvel though Demetrius
Do, as a monster, fly my presence thus.
What wicked and dissembling glass of mine
Made me compare with Hermia's sphery eyne?
But who is here? Lysander! On the ground!
Dead, or asleep? I see no blood, no wound.
Lysander, if you live, good sir, awake.

Hermia: "Help me, Lysander, help me! Do thy best"
[Act II, Scene 2]

{*Hermia, having eloped into the forest with Lysander, awakens from a nightmare expecting to find him beside her. (He has been charmed by a potion and is in love with Helena, after whom he has chased.)*}

Help me, Lysander, help me! Do thy best
To pluck this crawling serpent from my breast!
Ay me, for pity! What a dream was here!

Lysander, look how I do quake with fear:
Methought a serpent eat my heart away,
And you sat smiling at his cruel prey.
Lysander! What, removed? Lysander! Lord!
What, out of hearing? Gone? No sound, no word?
Alack, where are you? Speak, an if you hear.
Speak, of all loves! I swoon almost with fear.
No? Then I well perceive you all not nigh.
Either death or you I'll find immediately.

Helena: "O weary night, O long and tedious night" [Act III, Scene 2]

{Out in the forest, Helena, confused and feeling mocked by both Lysander's and Demetrius's charmed love for her, lies down to sleep.}

O weary night, O long and tedious night,
Abate thy hours! Shine comforts from the east,
That I may back to Athens by daylight,
From these that my poor company detest:
And sleep, that sometimes shuts up sorrow's eye,
Steal me awhile from mine own company.

Bottom: "When my cue comes, call me, and I will answer" [Act IV, Scene 1]

{Nick Bottom, a clownish weaver and amateur actor, awakes from a dream that was no dream at all. Calling to his fellow actors, nowhere to be seen, he is unable "to expound this dream" that (as a result of Puckish magic) he had an ass's head and was beloved by the queen of the fairies.}

When my cue comes, call me, and I will answer. My next is, "Most fair Pyramus." Heigh-ho! Peter Quince! Flute, the bellows-mender! Snout, the tinker! Starveling! God's my life, stolen hence, and left me asleep! I have had a most rare vision. I have had a dream, past the wit of man to say what dream it was. Man is but

an ass if he go about to expound this dream. Methought I was—
there is no man can tell what. Methought I was—and methought
I had—but man is but a patched fool if he will offer to say what
methought I had. The eye of man hath not heard, the ear of man
hath not seen, man's hand is not able to taste, his tongue to con-
ceive, nor his heart to report what my dream was. I will get Peter
Quince to write a ballad of this dream: it shall be called "Bottom's
Dream," because it hath no bottom; and I will sing it in the latter
end of our play, before the duke. Peradventure, to make it the more
gracious, I shall sing it at her death.

Pyramus: "Sweet Moon, I thank thee for thy sunny beams" [Act V, Scene 1]

{*The clownish Bottom, playing the melodramatic role of "Pyramus" in a
wedding entertainment before Theseus, the Duke of Athens, and Hippolyta, his
bride, believes his lover Thisby is dead and so kills himself. (Interspersed with
his soliloquy, Theseus and Hippolyta and the happy guests crack jokes at
Bottom's lines.)*}

Sweet Moon, I thank thee for thy sunny beams;
I thank thee, Moon, for shining now so bright;
For, by thy gracious, golden, glittering gleams,
I trust to take of truest Thisby sight.
But stay, O spite!
But mark, poor knight,
What dreadful dole is here!
Eyes, do you see?
How can it be?
O dainty duck! O dear!
Thy mantle good,
What, stain'd with blood!
Approach, ye Furies fell!
O Fates, come, come,
Cut thread and thrum;
Quail, crush, conclude, and quell!

O wherefore, Nature, didst thou lions frame?
Since lion vile hath here deflower'd my dear:

Which is—no, no—which was the fairest dame
That lived, that loved, that liked, that look'd with cheer.
Come, tears, confound;
Out, sword, and wound
The pap of Pyramus;
Ay, that left pap,
Where heart doth hop.

[*He stabs himself.*]

Thus die I, thus, thus, thus.
Now am I dead,
Now am I fled,
My soul is in the sky.
Tongue, lose thy light;
Moon, take thy flight:

Now die, die, die, die, die.

MUCH ADO ABOUT NOTHING

Benedick: "I do much wonder that one man, seeing how much another man is a fool when he dedicates his behaviors to love . . ." [Act II, Scene 3]

{*A young warrior of Aragon, Benedick, shakes his head at the folly of his friend Claudio, who has abandoned war for love.*}

I do much wonder that one man, seeing how much another man is a fool when he dedicates his behaviors to love, will, after he hath laughed at such shallow follies in others, become the argument of his own scorn by falling in love: and such a man is Claudio. I have known when there was no music with him but the drum and the fife; and now had he rather hear the tabor and the pipe. I have known when he would have walked ten mile a-foot to see a good armour; and now will he lie ten nights awake carving the fashion of a new doublet. He was wont to speak plain and to the purpose, like an honest man and a soldier; and now is he turned orthography; his words are a very fantastical banquet, just so many strange dishes. May I be so converted and see with these eyes? I cannot tell; I think not. I will not be sworn, but love may transform me to an oyster; but I'll take my oath on it, till he have made an oyster of me, he shall never make me such a fool. One woman is fair, yet I am well; another is wise, yet I am well; another virtuous, yet I am well; but till all graces be in one woman, one woman shall not come in my grace. Rich she shall be, that's certain; wise, or I'll none; virtuous, or I'll never cheapen her; fair, or I'll never look on her; mild, or come not near me; noble, or not I for an angel; of good discourse, an excellent musician, and her hair shall be of what colour it please God.

Benedick: "This can be no trick . . ." [Act II, Scene 3]

{*Having declared himself intellectually and emotionally superior to love, Benedick has been tricked (in spite of his leeriness) by his friends into believing that Beatrice, a young woman who has publicly renounced him and romance, is in love with him.*}

This can be no trick: the conference was sadly borne. They have the truth of this from Hero. They seem to pity the lady: it seems her affections have their full bent. Love me? Why, it must be requited. I hear how I am censured: they say I will bear myself proudly if I perceive the love come from her. They say too that she will rather die than give any sign of affection. I did never think to marry: I must not seem proud. Happy are they that hear their detractions and can put them to mending. They say the lady is fair; 'tis a truth, I can bear them witness; and virtuous; 'tis so, I cannot reprove it; and wise, but for loving me; by my troth, it is no addition to her wit, nor no great argument of her folly, for I will be horribly in love with her. I may chance have some odd quirks and remnants of wit broken on me, because I have railed so long against marriage. But doth not the appetite alter? A man loves the meat in his youth that he cannot endure in his age. Shall quips and sentences and these paper bullets of the brain awe a man from the career of his humour? No, the world must be peopled. When I said I would die a bachelor, I did not think I should live till I were married. Here comes Beatrice. By this day, she's a fair lady! I do spy some marks of love in her.

Beatrice: "What fire is in mine ears? Can this be true?"
[Act III, Scene 1]

{*The young beautiful Beatrice, her vehement denunciations of the power of love notwithstanding, has been guiled by her matchmaking friends into falling in love with her nemesis Benedick.*}

What fire is in mine ears? Can this be true?
Stand I condemn'd for pride and scorn so much?
Contempt, farewell! and maiden pride, adieu!
No glory lives behind the back of such.
And, Benedick, love on; I will requite thee,
Taming my wild heart to thy loving hand.
If thou dost love, my kindness shall incite thee
To bind our loves up in a holy band;
For others say thou dost deserve, and I
Believe it better than reportingly.

OTHELLO

Iago: "And what's he then that says I play the villain"
[Act II, Scene 3]

{*Everyone trusts Iago, especially Lieutenant Cassio and General Othello, both of whom he is intent upon destroying. Iago, Othello the Moor's ensign, despises his commander's moral and military superiority and means to poison Othello with jealousy against his innocent bride Desdemona, to whom Iago himself is attracted. Cassio puts his life in the hands of his advisor, whom he calls, to Iago's amusement at the irony, "honest."*}

And what's he then that says I play the villain,
When this advice is free I give and honest,
Probal to thinking, and indeed the course
To win the Moor again? For 'tis most easy
Th' inclining Desdemona to subdue
In any honest suit: she's framed as fruitful
As the free elements. And then for her
To win the Moor—were't to renounce his baptism,
All seals and symbols of redeemèd sin,
His soul is so enfetter'd to her love
That she may make, unmake, do what she list,
Even as her appetite shall play the god
With his weak function. How am I then a villain
To counsel Cassio to this parallel course,
Directly to his good? Divinity of hell!
When devils will the blackest sins put on,
They do suggest at first with heavenly shows,
As I do now: for whiles this honest fool
Plies Desdemona to repair his fortunes,
And she for him pleads strongly to the Moor,
I'll pour this pestilence into his ear,

That she repeals him for her body's lust;
And by how much she strives to do him good,
She shall undo her credit with the Moor.
So will I turn her virtue into pitch,
And out of her own goodness make the net
That shall enmesh them all.

Othello: "It is the cause, it is the cause, my soul"
[Act V, Scene 2]

{*Persuaded by Iago's suggestions that his wife has taken Cassio as a lover,
Othello enters Desdemona's chamber to murder her.*}

It is the cause, it is the cause, my soul.
Let me not name it to you, you chaste stars!
It is the cause. Yet I'll not shed her blood,
Nor scar that whiter skin of hers than snow,
And smooth as monumental alabaster.
Yet she must die, else she'll betray more men.
Put out the light, and then put out the light:
If I quench thee, thou flaming minister,
I can again thy former light restore,
Should I repent me: but once put out thy light,
Thou cunning'st pattern of excelling nature,
I know not where is that Promethean heat
That can thy light relume. When I have pluck'd the rose,
I cannot give it vital growth again.
It must needs wither: I'll smell thee on the tree.

[*He kisses her.*]

O balmy breath, that dost almost persuade
Justice to break her sword! One more, one more!
Be thus when thou art dead, and I will kill thee,
And love thee after. One more, and that's the last:
So sweet was ne'er so fatal. I must weep,
But they are cruel tears: this sorrow's heavenly;
It strikes where it doth love. She wakes.

PERICLES

Pericles: "Yet cease your ire, you angry stars of heaven!"
[Act II, Scene 1]

{*Pursued by a terrible king's assassin, Pericles has been shipwrecked near Pentapolis and curses Nature, though he will soon win here the hand of a beautiful princess.*}

Yet cease your ire, you angry stars of heaven!
Wind, rain, and thunder, remember, earthly man
Is but a substance that must yield to you;
And I, as fits my nature, do obey you.
Alas, the sea hath cast me on the rocks,
Wash'd me from shore to shore, and left me breath
Nothing to think on but ensuing death.
Let it suffice the greatness of your powers
To have bereft a prince of all his fortunes,
And having thrown him from your wat'ry grave,
Here to have death in peace is all he'll crave.

RICHARD II

Richard: "I have been studying how I may compare"
[Act V, Scene 5]

{*In prison in Pomfret Castle, Richard II, having relinquished his throne to Bolingbroke (now Henry IV), awaits his fate—which will soon come by way of assassination in his cell.*}

I have been studying how I may compare
This prison where I live unto the world:
And, for because the world is populous,
And here is not a creature but myself,
I cannot do it; yet I'll hammer it out.
My brain I'll prove the female to my soul,
My soul the father; and these two beget
A generation of still-breeding thoughts,
And these same thoughts people this little world,
In humours like the people of this world,
For no thought is contented. The better sort,
As thoughts of things divine, are intermix'd
With scruples, and do set the word itself
Against the word:
As thus, "Come, little ones," and then again,
"It is as hard to come as for a camel
To thread the postern of a small needle's eye."
Thoughts tending to ambition, they do plot
Unlikely wonders; how these vain weak nails
May tear a passage through the flinty ribs
Of this hard world, my ragged prison walls;
And, for they cannot, die in their own pride.
Thoughts tending to content flatter themselves

73

That they are not the first of fortune's slaves,
Nor shall not be the last; like silly beggars
Who sitting in the stocks refuge their shame,
That many have, and others must sit there.
And in this thought they find a kind of ease,
Bearing their own misfortunes on the back
Of such as have before endured the like.
Thus play I in one person many people,
And none contented. Sometimes am I king;
Then treasons make me wish myself a beggar,
And so I am. Then crushing penury
Persuades me I was better when a king;
Then am I king'd again: and by and by
Think that I am unking'd by Bolingbroke,
And straight am nothing. But whate'er I be,
Nor I, nor any man, that but man is
With nothing shall be pleased, till he be eased
With being nothing. [*Music plays.*] Music do I hear?
Ha, ha! Keep time. How sour sweet music is
When time is broke and no proportion kept!
So is it in the music of men's lives.
And here have I the daintiness of ear
To check time broke in a disorder'd string;
But, for the concord of my state and time,
Had not an ear to hear my true time broke.
I wasted time, and now doth time waste me;
For now hath time made me his numb'ring clock:
My thoughts are minutes; and with sighs they jar
Their watches on unto mine eyes, the outward watch,
Whereto my finger, like a dial's point,
Is pointing still, in cleansing them from tears.
Now, sir, the sound that tells what hour it is
Are clamorous groans, which strike upon my heart,
Which is the bell. So sighs and tears and groans
Show minutes, times, and hours: but my time
Runs posting on in Bolingbroke's proud joy,
While I stand fooling here, his Jack o' the clock.

This music mads me; let it sound no more;
For though it have holp madmen to their wits,
In me it seems it will make wise men mad.
Yet blessing on his heart that gives it me!
For 'tis a sign of love; and love to Richard
Is a strange brooch in this all-hating world.

RICHARD III

Richard: "Now is the winter of our discontent"
[Act I, Scene 1]

{*Richard Plantagenet of York, the Duke of Gloucester, opens this play reviewing his situation. As the brother of the king, Edward IV, he means to continue disposing of the others in line for the throne, including their brother George, the Duke of Clarence.*}

Now is the winter of our discontent
Made glorious summer by this sun of York;
And all the clouds that lour'd upon our house
In the deep bosom of the ocean buried.
Now are our brows bound with victorious wreaths;
Our bruisèd arms hung up for monuments;
Our stern alarums changed to merry meetings;
Our dreadful marches to delightful measures.
Grim-visaged war hath smooth'd his wrinkled front;
And now, instead of mounting barbèd steeds
To fright the souls of fearful adversaries,
He capers nimbly in a lady's chamber
To the lascivious pleasing of a lute.
But I, that am not shaped for sportive tricks,
Nor made to court an amorous looking-glass;
I, that am rudely stamp'd, and want love's majesty
To strut before a wanton ambling nymph;
I, that am curtail'd of this fair proportion,
Cheated of feature by dissembling nature,
Deform'd, unfinish'd, sent before my time
Into this breathing world, scarce half made up,
And that so lamely and unfashionable
That dogs bark at me as I halt by them;

Why I, in this weak piping time of peace,
Have no delight to pass away the time,
Unless to spy my shadow in the sun
And descant on mine own deformity:
And therefore, since I cannot prove a lover
To entertain these fair well-spoken days,
I am determinèd to prove a villain
And hate the idle pleasures of these days.
Plots have I laid, inductions dangerous,
By drunken prophecies, libels, and dreams,
To set my brother Clarence and the king
In deadly hate the one against the other:
And if King Edward be as true and just
As I am subtle, false, and treacherous,
This day should Clarence closely be mew'd up,
About a prophecy, which says that "G"
Of Edward's heirs the murderer shall be.
Dive, thoughts, down to my soul: here Clarence comes.

Richard: "Was ever woman in this humour wooed?"
[Act I, Scene 2]

{*Richard, still Duke of Gloucester, relishes the idea of marrying the woman whose husband (Prince Edward) and father-in-law (Henry VI) he murdered. Her status, he believes, will help him gain the throne when Edward IV dies.*}

Was ever woman in this humour wooed?
Was ever woman in this humour won?
I'll have her; but I will not keep her long.
What! I, that kill'd her husband and his father,
To take her in her heart's extremest hate,
With curses in her mouth, tears in her eyes,
The bleeding witness of her hatred by;
Having God, her conscience, and these bars against me,
And I nothing to back my suit at all
But the plain devil and dissembling looks?
And yet to win her, all the world to nothing!
Ha!

Hath she forgot already that brave prince,
Edward, her lord, whom I, some three months since,
Stabb'd in my angry mood at Tewksbury?
A sweeter and a lovelier gentleman,
Framed in the prodigality of nature,
Young, valiant, wise, and, no doubt, right royal,
The spacious world cannot again afford;
And will she yet debase her eyes on me,
That cropp'd the golden prime of this sweet prince,
And made her widow to a woeful bed?
On me, whose all not equals Edward's moiety?
On me, that halts and am unshapen thus?
My dukedom to a beggarly denier,
I do mistake my person all this while:
Upon my life, she finds, although I cannot,
Myself to be a marv'llous proper man.
I'll be at charges for a looking-glass,
And entertain a score or two of tailors,
To study fashions to adorn my body:
Since I am crept in favour with myself,
I will maintain it with some little cost.
But first I'll turn yon fellow in his grave,
And then return lamenting to my love.
Shine out, fair sun, till I have bought a glass,
That I may see my shadow as I pass.

Richard: "Give me another horse! Bind up my wounds!"
[Act V, Scene 3]

{*In his army's camp, preparing to turn back the Lancastrian forces, Richard III, King of England, visited by ghosts in his dreams, wakes with a start. It is the night before he will be killed in the field at Bosworth by Richmond (Henry VII).*}

Give me another horse! Bind up my wounds!
Have mercy, Jesu!—Soft! I did but dream.
O coward conscience, how dost thou afflict me!
The lights burn blue. It is now dead midnight.

Cold fearful drops stand on my trembling flesh.
What do I fear? Myself? There's none else by:
Richard loves Richard; that is, I am I.
Is there a murderer here? No. Yes, I am:
Then fly. What, from myself? Great reason why:
Lest I revenge. What, myself upon myself?
Alack, I love myself. Wherefore? For any good
That I myself have done unto myself?
O, no! alas, I rather hate myself
For hateful deeds committed by myself!
I am a villain: yet I lie. I am not.
Fool, of thyself speak well: fool, do not flatter.
My conscience hath a thousand several tongues,
And every tongue brings in a several tale,
And every tale condemns me for a villain.
Perjury, perjury, in the high'st degree
Murder, stern murder, in the direst degree;
All several sins, all used in each degree,
Throng to the bar, crying all, "Guilty! guilty!"
I shall despair. There is no creature loves me;
And if I die, no soul shall pity me:
Nay, wherefore should they, since that I myself
Find in myself no pity to myself?
Methought the souls of all that I had murder'd
Came to my tent; and every one did threat
Tomorrow's vengeance on the head of Richard.

ROMEO AND JULIET

Romeo: "But, soft! What light through yonder window breaks?" [Act II, Scene 2]

{*Romeo Montague is secretly in love with Juliet Capulet, daughter of his family's enemy. At night, in the orchard beside the Capulets' house, Romeo sees her above at her window.*}

But, soft! What light through yonder window breaks?
It is the east, and Juliet is the sun!
Arise, fair sun, and kill the envious moon,
Who is already sick and pale with grief,
That thou her maid art far more fair than she:
Be not her maid, since she is envious;
Her vestal livery is but sick and green
And none but fools do wear it; cast it off.
It is my lady; O, it is my love!
O, that she knew she were!
She speaks, yet she says nothing: what of that?
Her eye discourses; I will answer it.
I am too bold, 'tis not to me she speaks:
Two of the fairest stars in all the heaven,
Having some business, do intreat her eyes
To twinkle in their spheres till they return.
What if her eyes were there, they in her head?
The brightness of her cheek would shame those stars,
As daylight doth a lamp; her eyes in heaven
Would through the airy region stream so bright
That birds would sing and think it were not night.
See, how she leans her cheek upon her hand!

O, that I were a glove upon that hand,
That I might touch that cheek!

She speaks!
O, speak again, bright angel! For thou art
As glorious to this night, being o'er my head,
As is a winged messenger of heaven
Unto the white-upturned wondering eyes
Of mortals that fall back to gaze on him,
When he bestrides the lazy-pacing clouds
And sails upon the bosom of the air.

Juliet: "O Romeo, Romeo! wherefore art thou Romeo?" [Act II, Scene 2]

{*Juliet, continuing the scene from the previous soliloquy, is struggling with the idea that she is in love with her family's enemy's son. (Young actors sometimes forget that Juliet's "wherefore" means "why.")*}

O Romeo, Romeo! wherefore art thou Romeo?
Deny thy father and refuse thy name;
Or, if thou wilt not, be but sworn my love,
And I'll no longer be a Capulet.

'Tis but thy name that is my enemy;
Thou art thyself, though not a Montague.
What's Montague? it is nor hand, nor foot,
Nor arm, nor face, nor any other part
Belonging to a man. O, be some other name!
What's in a name? That which we call a rose
By any other name would smell as sweet;
So Romeo would, were he not Romeo call'd,
Retain that dear perfection which he owes
Without that title. Romeo, doff thy name,
And for thy name which is no part of thee,
Take all myself.

Friar Laurence: "The grey-eyed morn smiles on the frowning night" [Act II, Scene 3]

{*Romeo's friend and confessor as yet knows nothing of Romeo's love for Juliet. (He will support them in hopes that their love will end their families' feud.) Entering his cell, he reflects on life's double-nature. (His knowledge of herbal medicine will help and then unfortunately harm Romeo and Juliet.)*}

The grey-eyed morn smiles on the frowning night,
Checkering the eastern clouds with streaks of light;
And flecked darkness like a drunkard reels
From forth day's path and Titan's fiery wheels:
Now, ere the sun advance his burning eye,
The day to cheer and night's dank dew to dry,
I must up-fill this osier cage of ours
With baleful weeds and precious-juiced flowers.
The earth that's nature's mother is her tomb;
What is her burying grave, that is her womb,
And from her womb children of divers kind
We sucking on her natural bosom find,
Many for many virtues excellent,
None but for some, and yet all different.
O, mickle is the powerful grace that lies
In herbs, plants, stones, and their true qualities:
For nought so vile that on the earth doth live
But to the earth some special good doth give;
Nor aught so good but strain'd from that fair use,
Revolts from true birth, stumbling on abuse:
Virtue itself turns vice, being misapplied,
And vice sometimes by action dignified.
Within the infant rind of this small flower
Poison hath residence and medicine power:
For this, being smelt, with that part cheers each part;
Being tasted, slays all senses with the heart.
Two such opposèd kings encamp them still
In man as well as herbs, grace and rude will;
And where the worser is predominant,
Full soon the canker death eats up that plant.

Juliet: "Gallop apace, you fiery-footed steeds"
[Act III, Scene 2]

{Anticipating her wedding with Romeo, Juliet apostrophizes "Night," impatient for night and Romeo to appear.}

Gallop apace, you fiery-footed steeds,
Towards Phoebus' lodging: such a wagoner
As Phaethon would whip you to the west,
And bring in cloudy night immediately.
Spread thy close curtain, love-performing night,
That runaways' eyes may wink and Romeo
Leap to these arms, untalk'd of and unseen.
Lovers can see to do their amorous rites
By their own beauties; or, if love be blind,
It best agrees with night. Come, civil night,
Thou sober-suited matron, all in black,
And learn me how to lose a winning match,
Play'd for a pair of stainless maidenhoods:
Hood my unmann'd blood, bating in my cheeks,
With thy black mantle, till strange love, grown bold,
Think true love acted simple modesty.
Come, night; come, Romeo; come, thou day in night;
For thou wilt lie upon the wings of night
Whiter than new snow on a raven's back.
Come, gentle night, come, loving, black-brow'd night,
Give me my Romeo; and, when he shall die,
Take him and cut him out in little stars,
And he will make the face of heaven so fine
That all the world will be in love with night
And pay no worship to the garish sun.
O! I have bought the mansion of a love,
But not possess'd it, and, though I am sold,
Not yet enjoy'd; so tedious is this day
As is the night before some festival
To an impatient child that hath new robes
And may not wear them. O, here comes my nurse,
And she brings news, and every tongue that speaks
But Romeo's name speaks heavenly eloquence.

Juliet: "Farewell! God knows when we shall meet again"
[Act IV, Scene 3]

{Juliet, secretly married to Romeo by Friar Laurence, is expected by her parents to marry her kinsman Paris in the morning. She has sent her nurse and mother out of the room so that she can take the friar's remedy that will render her death-like and allow her to escape with Romeo from her family's tomb.}

Farewell! God knows when we shall meet again.
I have a faint cold fear thrills through my veins,
That almost freezes up the heat of life:
I'll call them back again to comfort me.
Nurse!—What should she do here?
My dismal scene I needs must act alone.
Come, vial.
What if this mixture do not work at all?
Shall I be married then tomorrow morning?
No, no: this shall forbid it. Lie thou there.

[She lays down a dagger.]

What if it be a poison, which the friar
Subtly hath minister'd to have me dead,
Lest in this marriage he should be dishonour'd,
Because he married me before to Romeo?
I fear it is: and yet, methinks, it should not,
For he hath still been tried a holy man.
How if, when I am laid into the tomb,
I wake before the time that Romeo
Come to redeem me? There's a fearful point!
Shall I not, then, be stifled in the vault,
To whose foul mouth no healthsome air breathes in,
And there die strangled ere my Romeo comes?
Or, if I live, is it not very like,
The horrible conceit of death and night,
Together with the terror of the place,
As in a vault, an ancient receptacle,
Where, for this many hundred years, the bones
Of all my buried ancestors are pack'd:
Where bloody Tybalt, yet but green in earth,
Lies festering in his shroud; where, as they say,

At some hours in the night spirits resort;
Alack, alack, is it not like that I
So early waking, what with loathsome smells
And shrieks like mandrakes' torn out of the earth,
That living mortals, hearing them, run mad:
O, if I wake, shall I not be distraught,
Environed with all these hideous fears?
And madly play with my forefathers' joints?
And pluck the mangled Tybalt from his shroud?
And, in this rage, with some great kinsman's bone,
As with a club, dash out my desperate brains?
O, look! methinks I see my cousin's ghost
Seeking out Romeo, that did spit his body
Upon a rapier's point: stay, Tybalt, stay!
Romeo, I come! This do I drink to thee.

[*She falls upon her bed, within the curtains.*]

Romeo: "If I may trust the flattering truth of sleep"
[Act V, Scene 1]

{*Romeo, in exile in Mantua for having killed Tybalt, Juliet's cousin, cheerfully awaits her arrival and their happiness. His dream is an ironic mixture of prophecy and misunderstanding.*}

If I may trust the flattering truth of sleep,
My dreams presage some joyful news at hand:
My bosom's lord sits lightly in his throne;
And all this day an unaccustom'd spirit
Lifts me above the ground with cheerful thoughts.
I dreamt my lady came and found me dead—
Strange dream, that gives a dead man leave to think!—
And breathed such life with kisses in my lips,
That I revived and was an emperor.
Ah me! how sweet is love itself possess'd,
When but love's shadows are so rich in joy!

Romeo: "Let me peruse this face" [Act V, Scene 3]

{*Entering the Capulet family's tomb, Romeo encounters Paris, who attacks him. Romeo kills him, then lays him down in the tomb and sees Juliet, who seems dead but is only unconscious from the friar's drug. (Romeo did not receive Friar Laurence's letter informing him of this ruse.) Lamenting Juliet, Romeo then takes his own fatal poison.*}

Let me peruse this face:
Mercutio's kinsman, noble County Paris!
What said my man, when my betossèd soul
Did not attend him as we rode? I think
He told me Paris should have married Juliet:
Said he not so? Or did I dream it so?
Or am I mad, hearing him talk of Juliet,
To think it was so? O, give me thy hand,
One writ with me in sour misfortune's book!
I'll bury thee in a triumphant grave;
A grave? O no; a lantern, slaughter'd youth;
For here lies Juliet, and her beauty makes
This vault a feasting presence full of light.
Death, lie thou there, by a dead man interr'd.

[*He places Paris in the tomb.*]

How oft when men are at the point of death
Have they been merry! which their keepers call
A lightning before death: O, how may I
Call this a lightning? O my love! my wife!
Death, that hath suck'd the honey of thy breath,
Hath had no power yet upon thy beauty:
Thou art not conquer'd; beauty's ensign yet
Is crimson in thy lips and in thy cheeks,
And death's pale flag is not advanced there.
Tybalt, liest thou there in thy bloody sheet?
O, what more favour can I do to thee,
Than with that hand that cut thy youth in twain
To sunder his that was thine enemy?
Forgive me, cousin! Ah, dear Juliet,
Why art thou yet so fair? Shall I believe
That unsubstantial death is amorous,

And that the lean abhorrèd monster keeps
Thee here in dark to be his paramour?
For fear of that, I still will stay with thee,
And never from this palace of dim night
Depart again: here, here will I remain
With worms that are thy chamber-maids. O, here
Will I set up my everlasting rest,
And shake the yoke of inauspicious stars
From this world-wearied flesh. Eyes, look your last!
Arms, take your last embrace! and, lips, O you
The doors of breath, seal with a righteous kiss
A dateless bargain to engrossing death!
Come, bitter conduct, come, unsavoury guide!
Thou desperate pilot, now at once run on
The dashing rocks thy seasick weary bark!
Here's to my love!

[*He drinks.*]

O true apothecary!
Thy drugs are quick. Thus with a kiss I die.

THE TAMING OF THE SHREW

Petruchio: "Thus have I politicly begun my reign"
[Act IV, Scene 1]

{*A bold young man of Verona, Petruchio goes to Padua, where, tempted by the wealth of Baptista Minola, agrees to take on Katherine, Baptista's ill-tempered daughter, as his wife. He out-savages Kate and thus tames her. Here he reviews his method.*}

Thus have I politicly begun my reign,
And 'tis my hope to end successfully.
My falcon now is sharp and passing empty;
And till she stoop she must not be full-gorged,
For then she never looks upon her lure.
Another way I have to man my haggard,
To make her come and know her keeper's call:
That is, to watch her as we watch these kites
That bate and beat and will not be obedient.
She eat no meat today, nor none shall eat;
Last night she slept not, nor tonight she shall not;
As with the meat, some undeservèd fault
I'll find about the making of the bed;
And here I'll fling the pillow, there the bolster,
This way the coverlet, another way the sheets.
Ay, and amid this hurly I intend
That all is done in reverend care of her;
And in conclusion she shall watch all night:
And if she chance to nod I'll rail and brawl
And with the clamour keep her still awake.
This is a way to kill a wife with kindness;
And thus I'll curb her mad and headstrong humour.
He that knows better how to tame a shrew,
Now let him speak: 'tis charity to show.

THE TEMPEST

Caliban: "All the infections that the sun sucks up"
[Act II, Scene 2]

{ *"A freckled whelp, hag-born," as described by his overbearing master Prospero, the misshapen Caliban, bearing firewood under a looming storm, resents his lonely servitude on his island, and, in spite of his awareness of Prospero's fairy spies, laments his fate. He hides at the approach of Prospero's jester, Trinculo.*}

All the infections that the sun sucks up
From bogs, fens, flats, on Prosper fall, and make him
By inch-meal a disease! His spirits hear me
And yet I needs must curse. But they'll nor pinch,
Fright me with urchin-shows, pitch me i' the mire,
Nor lead me, like a firebrand, in the dark
Out of my way, unless he bid 'em; but
For every trifle are they set upon me,
Sometime like apes that mow and chatter at me
And after bite me, then like hedgehogs which
Lie tumbling in my barefoot way and mount
Their pricks at my footfall; sometime am I
All wound with adders, who with cloven tongues
Do hiss me into madness.

[*Enter Trinculo.*]

                              Lo, now, lo!
Here comes a spirit of his, and to torment me
For bringing wood in slowly. I'll fall flat:
Perchance he will not mind me.

Ferdinand: "There be some sports are painful, and their labour" [Act III, Scene 1]

{*The prince of Milan, Ferdinand, is in love with Miranda, Prospero's daughter. To prove his mettle, Prospero has set him to work.*}

There be some sports are painful, and their labour
Delight in them sets off; some kinds of baseness
Are nobly undergone, and most poor matters
Point to rich ends. This my mean task
Would be as heavy to me as odious, but
The mistress which I serve quickens what's dead
And makes my labours pleasures. O, she is
Ten times more gentle than her father's crabbèd,
And he's composed of harshness! I must remove
Some thousands of these logs and pile them up,
Upon a sore injunction. My sweet mistress
Weeps when she sees me work, and says such baseness
Had never like executor. I forget:
But these sweet thoughts do even refresh my labours,
Most busy lest, when I do it.

TIMON OF ATHENS

Alcibiades: "Now the gods keep you old enough; that you may live" [Act III, Scene 5]

{The Athenian senate has denied the great general the favor of staying the execution of a friend. So outraged is Alcibiades that his words provoke the senate into banishing him from Athens. He vows vengeance.}

Now the gods keep you old enough; that you may live
Only in bone, that none may look on you!
I am worse than mad: I have kept back their foes,
While they have told their money and let out
Their coin upon large interest; I myself
Rich only in large hurts. All those for this?
Is this the balsam that the usuring senate
Pours into captains' wounds? Banishment!
It comes not ill; I hate not to be banish'd;
It is a cause worthy my spleen and fury,
That I may strike at Athens. I'll cheer up
My discontented troops, and lay for hearts.
'Tis honour with most lands to be at odds;
Soldiers should brook as little wrongs as gods.

Timon: "Let me look back upon thee. O thou wall" [Act IV, Scene 1]

{Timon is Athens' most generous nobleman, distributing favors and money and hosting parties. When his money runs out, so do almost all of his friends, and after telling off those friends, he curses Athens and leaves in disgust and disappointment.}

91

Let me look back upon thee. O thou wall,
That girdlest in those wolves, dive in the earth,
And fence not Athens! Matrons, turn incontinent!
Obedience fail in children! Slaves and fools,
Pluck the grave wrinkled senate from the bench,
And minister in their steads! To general filths
Convert o' the instant, green virginity!
Do 't in your parents' eyes! Bankrupts, hold fast;
Rather than render back, out with your knives,
And cut your trusters' throats! Bound servants, steal!
Large-handed robbers your grave masters are,
And pill by law. Maid, to thy master's bed;
Thy mistress is o' the brothel! Son of sixteen,
Pluck the lin'd crutch from thy old limping sire,
With it beat out his brains! Piety, and fear,
Religion to the gods, peace, justice, truth,
Domestic awe, night-rest, and neighbourhood,
Instruction, manners, mysteries, and trades,
Degrees, observances, customs, and laws,
Decline to your confounding contraries,
And let confusion live! Plagues, incident to men,
Your potent and infectious fevers heap
On Athens, ripe for stroke! Thou cold sciatica,
Cripple our senators, that their limbs may halt
As lamely as their manners! Lust and liberty
Creep in the minds and marrows of our youth,
That 'gainst the stream of virtue they may strive,
And drown themselves in riot! Itches, blains,
Sow all the Athenian bosoms; and their crop
Be general leprosy! Breath infect breath,
That their society, as their friendship, may
Be merely poison! Nothing I'll bear from thee,
But nakedness, thou detestable town!
Take thou that too, with multiplying bans!
Timon will to the woods; where he shall find
The unkindest beast more kinder than mankind.
The gods confound—hear me, you good gods all—
The Athenians both within and out that wall!

And grant, as Timon grows, his hate may grow
To the whole race of mankind, high and low!
Amen.

Flavius: "O, the fierce wretchedness that glory brings us!" [Act IV, Scene 2]

{*Timon's true and honest steward, Flavius, who tried to protect Timon from excesses of generosity, has shared some of his remaining money with Timon's servants. Bidding them farewell, he leaves Timon's house to search for Timon in the woods.*}

O, the fierce wretchedness that glory brings us!
Who would not wish to be from wealth exempt,
Since riches point to misery and contempt?
Who would be so mock'd with glory? or to live
But in a dream of friendship?
To have his pomp and all what state compounds
But only painted, like his varnish'd friends?
Poor honest lord, brought low by his own heart,
Undone by goodness! Strange, unusual blood,
When man's worst sin is, he does too much good!
Who, then, dares to be half so kind again?
For bounty, that makes gods, does still mar men.
My dearest lord, bless'd, to be most accurs'd,
Rich, only to be wretched, thy great fortunes
Are made thy chief afflictions. Alas, kind lord!
He's flung in rage from this ingrateful seat
Of monstrous friends;
Nor has he with him to supply his life,
Or that which can command it.
I'll follow and inquire him out:
I'll ever serve his mind with my best will;
Whilst I have gold, I'll be his steward still.

Timon: "O blessed breeding sun! Draw from the earth"
[Act IV, Scene 3]

{*Timon, the maddened, resentful nobleman who renounced his native Athens to live in the woods, comes out from his cave and begins the work of digging for edible roots. Instead, he discovers buried treasure.*}

O blessed breeding sun! Draw from the earth
Rotten humidity; below thy sister's orb
Infect the air! Twinn'd brothers of one womb,
Whose procreation, residence, and birth,
Scarce is dividant, touch them with several fortunes;
The greater scorns the lesser: not nature,
To whom all sores lay siege, can bear great fortune,
But by contempt of nature.
Raise me this beggar, and deny 't that lord;
The senator shall bear contempt hereditary,
The beggar native honour.
It is the pasture lards the rother's sides,
The want that makes him lean. Who dares, who dares,
In purity of manhood stand upright,
And say "This man's a flatterer"? If one be,
So are they all; for every grize of fortune
Is smooth'd by that below: the learnèd pate
Ducks to the golden fool: all is oblique;
There's nothing level in our cursed natures,
But direct villainy. Therefore, be abhorr'd
All feasts, societies, and throngs of men!
His semblable, yea, himself, Timon disdains:
Destruction fang mankind! Earth, yield me roots!

[*He digs.*]

Who seeks for better of thee, sauce his palate
With thy most operant poison! What is here?
Gold? Yellow, glittering, precious gold! No, gods,
I am no idle votarist: roots, you clear heavens!
Thus much of this will make black white, foul fair,
Wrong right, base noble, old young, coward valiant.
Ha, you gods! Why this? What this, you gods? Why, this
Will lug your priests and servants from your sides,

Pluck stout men's pillows from below their heads:
This yellow slave
Will knit and break religions, bless the accursed,
Make the hoar leprosy adored, place thieves
And give them title, knee, and approbation
With senators on the bench: this is it
That makes the wappen'd widow wed again;
She, whom the spital-house and ulcerous sores
Would cast the gorge at, this embalms and spices
To the April day again. Come, damned earth,
Thou common whore of mankind, that puts odds
Among the rout of nations, I will make thee
Do thy right nature.

[*The sound of a march far off.*]

Ha! A drum? Thou'rt quick,
But yet I'll bury thee: thou'lt go, strong thief,
When gouty keepers of thee cannot stand.
Nay, stay thou out for earnest.

TROILUS AND CRESSIDA

Troilus: "Peace, you ungracious clamours! Peace, rude sounds!" [Act I, Scene 1]

{*In the midst of the Trojan War, Troilus, one of the sons of King Priam of Troy, has fallen in love with Cressida. Troilus has confessed his love for Cressida to her uncle, Pandarus, who will help bring the lovers together.*}

Peace, you ungracious clamours! Peace, rude sounds!
Fools on both sides! Helen must needs be fair,
When with your blood you daily paint her thus.
I cannot fight upon this argument;
It is too starved a subject for my sword.
But Pandarus—O gods, how do you plague me!
I cannot come to Cressid but by Pandar;
And he's as tetchy to be woo'd to woo
As she is stubborn, chaste against all suit.
Tell me, Apollo, for thy Daphne's love,
What Cressid is, what Pandar, and what we?
Her bed is India; there she lies, a pearl:
Between our Ilium and where she resides,
Let it be call'd the wild and wand'ring flood,
Ourself the merchant, and this sailing Pandar
Our doubtful hope, our convoy, and our bark.

Cressida: "Words, vows, gifts, tears, and love's full sacrifice" [Act I, Scene 2]

{*Her uncle Pandarus has tried to persuade her to consider accepting the love of Troilus, the Trojan hero. They have watched him pass by with the army, but Cressida has pretended to her uncle not to be interested.*}

Words, vows, gifts, tears, and love's full sacrifice,
He offers in another's enterprise;
But more in Troilus thousand fold I see
Than in the glass of Pandar's praise may be;
Yet hold I off. Women are angels, wooing:
Things won are done; joy's soul lies in the doing.
That she beloved knows nought that knows not this:
Men prize the thing ungain'd more than it is:
That she was never yet that ever knew
Love got so sweet as when desire did sue.
Therefore this maxim out of love I teach:
Achievement is command; ungain'd, beseech:
Then though my heart's content firm love doth bear,
Nothing of that shall from mine eyes appear.

Troilus: "I am giddy; expectation whirls me round" [Act III, Scene 2]

{*Overwhelmed by his feelings, Troilus awaits Pandarus's return with Cressida, with whom Troilus will meet in private for the first time. (Soon after this "honeymoon," her father will arrange for her transfer to the Greeks' side, where the great warrior Diomedes will woo and love her.)*}

I am giddy; expectation whirls me round.
The imaginary relish is so sweet
That it enchants my sense. What will it be
When that the watery palate tastes indeed
Love's thrice-repurèd nectar? Death, I fear me,
Swooning destruction, or some joy too fine,
Too subtle-potent, tuned too sharp in sweetness,
For the capacity of my ruder powers:
I fear it much; and I do fear besides
That I shall lose distinction in my joys,
As doth a battle, when they charge on heaps
The enemy flying.

TWELFTH NIGHT

Olivia: " 'What is your parentage?' " [Act I, Scene 5]

{*Olivia, a countess who has rejected Count Orsino's wooing, finds herself won by his emissary, "Cesario," who, unknown to the count or Olivia, is Violet, in disguise, and herself in love with Orsino.*}

"What is your parentage?"
"Above my fortunes, yet my state is well:
I am a gentleman." I'll be sworn thou art.
Thy tongue, thy face, thy limbs, actions, and spirit,
Do give thee five-fold blazon: not too fast: soft, soft!
Unless the master were the man. How now!
Even so quickly may one catch the plague?
Methinks I feel this youth's perfections
With an invisible and subtle stealth
To creep in at mine eyes. Well, let it be.

Violet: "I left no ring with her: what means this lady?" [Act II, Scene 2]

{*Malvolio, the Countess Olivia's foolish steward, has chased after Violet (who in her disguise seems to all to be a young handsome man named Cesario), and "returned" to her a ring that Olivia told Malvolio Cesario left behind.*}

I left no ring with her: what means this lady?
Fortune forbid my outside have not charm'd her!
She made good view of me; indeed, so much,
That methought her eyes had lost her tongue,
For she did speak in starts distractedly.

She loves me, sure; the cunning of her passion
Invites me in this churlish messenger.
None of my lord's ring! Why, he sent her none.
I am the man. If it be so, as 'tis,
Poor lady, she were better love a dream.
Disguise, I see, thou art a wickedness,
Wherein the pregnant enemy does much.
How easy is it for the proper-false
In women's waxen hearts to set their forms!
Alas, our frailty is the cause, not we!
For such as we are made of, such we be.
How will this fadge? My master loves her dearly;
And I, poor monster, fond as much on him;
And she, mistaken, seems to dote on me.
What will become of this? As I am man,
My state is desperate for my master's love;
As I am woman—now alas the day!—
What thriftless sighs shall poor Olivia breathe?
O time! thou must untangle this, not I;
It is too hard a knot for me t' untie!

Malvolio: "'Tis but fortune; all is fortune" [Act II, Scene 5]

{*The Countess Olivia's steward becomes the butt of a practical joke played on him by Olivia's maid Maria. He has fantasized that Olivia will fall in love with him, and he finds a letter, apparently from her, that fulfills that fantasy. In the course of this soliloquy, undetected by him, he is observed and mocked by Maria, Olivia's uncle Sir Toby Belch, and another rogue, Andrew Aguecheek, who is himself courting Olivia.*}

'Tis but fortune; all is fortune. Maria once told me she did affect me: and I have heard herself come thus near, that, should she fancy, it should be one of my complexion. Besides, she uses me with a more exalted respect than anyone else that follows her. What should I think on 't?

To be Count Malvolio!

There is example for 't; the lady of the Strachy married the yeoman of the wardrobe. Having been three months married to her, sitting in my state, calling my officers about me, in my branched velvet gown; having come from a day-bed, where I have left Olivia sleeping, and then to have the humour of the state; and after a demure travel of regard, telling them I know my place as I would they should do theirs, to ask for my kinsman Toby. Seven of my people, with an obedient start, make out for him: I frown the while; and perchance wind up my watch, or play with my—some rich jewel. Toby approaches; courtesies there to me, I extend my hand to him thus, quenching my familiar smile with an austere regard of control, saying, "Cousin Toby, my fortunes having cast me on your niece, give me this prerogative of speech. You must amend your drunkenness. Besides, you waste the treasure of your time with a foolish knight, one Sir Andrew."

[*Malvolio sees the letter that Maria has forged from Olivia to him.*]

What employment have we here?

By my life, this is my lady's hand; these be her very C's, her U's, and her T's; and thus makes she her great P's. It is, in contempt of question, her hand.

[*He reads the letter.*]

"To the unknown beloved, this, and my good wishes"—her very phrases! By your leave, wax. Soft! And the impressure her Lucrece, with which she uses to seal: 'tis my lady. To whom should this be?

"Jove knows I love:
But who?
Lips do not move;
No man must know."

"No man must know." What follows? The numbers altered! "No man must know." If this should be thee, Malvolio?

"I may command where I adore;
But silence, like a Lucrece knife,
With bloodless stroke my heart doth gore:
M, O, A, I, doth sway my life."

"M, O, A, I, doth sway my life." Nay, but first, let me see, let me see, let me see. "I may command where I adore." Why, she may command me; I serve her; she is my lady. Why, this is evident to

any formal capacity; there is no obstruction in this: and the end—
what should that alphabetical position portend? If I could make
that resemble something in me.—Softly! M, O, A, I.

M—Malvolio; *M*—why, that begins my name. *M*—but then
there is no consonancy in the sequel; that suffers under probation:
A should follow, but *O* does. And then *I* comes behind. M, O, A,
I; this simulation is not as the former: and yet, to crush this a little,
it would bow to me, for every one of these letters are in my name.
Soft! Here follows prose.

"If this fall into thy hand, resolve. In my stars I am above thee;
but be not afraid of greatness: some are born great, some achieve
greatness, and some have greatness thrust upon 'em. Thy Fates
open their hands; let thy blood and spirit embrace them; and, to
inure thyself to what thou art like to be, cast thy humble slough
and appear fresh. Be opposite with a kinsman, surly with servants;
let thy tongue tang arguments of state; put thyself into the trick of
singularity: she thus advises thee that sighs for thee. Remember
who commended thy yellow stockings, and wished to see thee ever
cross-gartered: I say, remember. Go to, thou art made, if thou de-
sirest to be so; if not, let me see thee a steward still, the fellow of
servants, and not worthy to touch Fortune's fingers. Farewell. She
that would alter services with thee,

"THE FORTUNATE-UNHAPPY"

Daylight and champain discovers not more; this is open. I will
be proud, I will read politic authors, I will baffle Sir Toby, I will
wash off gross acquaintance, I will be point-devise the very man. I
do not now fool myself, to let imagination jade me; for every reason excites to this, that my lady loves me. She did commend my
yellow stockings of late, she did praise my leg being cross-gartered;
and in this she manifests herself to my love, and with a kind of injunction drives me to these habits of her liking. I thank my stars I
am happy. I will be strange, stout, in yellow stockings, and cross-
gartered, even with the swiftness of putting on. Jove and my stars
be praised! Here is yet a postscript.

"Thou canst not choose but know who I am. If thou enter-
tainest my love, let it appear in thy smiling; thy smiles become thee
well; therefore in my presence still smile, dear my sweet, I prithee."

Jove, I thank thee: I will smile; I will do everything that thou wilt
have me.

Violet: "This fellow's wise enough to play the fool"
[Act III, Scene 1]

{*Having conversed with Olivia's clown Feste, Viola makes a discovery that shows her own quick and witty mind.*}

This fellow's wise enough to play the fool,
And to do that well craves a kind of wit:
He must observe their mood on whom he jests,
The quality of persons, and the time,
And, like the haggard, check at every feather
That comes before his eye. This is a practice
As full of labour as a wise man's art;
For folly that he wisely shows is fit;
But wise men folly-fall'n quite taint their wit.

Sebastian: "This is the air; that is the glorious sun"
[Act IV, Scene 3]

{*Sebastian, Violet's lost (and believed drowned) twin brother, has shown up in Illyria and been mistaken by Olivia for her beloved "Cesario" (Violet-in-disguise). He wonders at the world's confusion.*}

This is the air; that is the glorious sun;
This pearl she gave me, I do feel't and see't;
And though 'tis wonder that enwraps me thus,
Yet 'tis not madness. Where's Antonio, then?
I could not find him at the Elephant:
Yet there he was; and there I found this credit,
That he did range the town to seek me out.
His counsel now might do me golden service;
For though my soul disputes well with my sense,
That this may be some error, but no madness,
Yet doth this accident and flood of fortune
So far exceed all instance, all discourse,
That I am ready to distrust mine eyes
And wrangle with my reason that persuades me
To any other trust but that I am mad
Or else the lady's mad. Yet, if 'twere so,

She could not sway her house, command her followers,
Take and give back affairs and their dispatch
With such a smooth, discreet, and stable bearing
As I perceive she does. There's something in't
That is deceiveable. But here the lady comes.

THE TWO GENTLEMEN OF VERONA

Julia: "Nay, would I were so anger'd with the same!"
[Act I, Scene 2]

{*In a fit of pique over the correct opinion of her waiting woman that Proteus is just the man for her, Julia rips up his love letter. Alone, she regrets her behavior.*}

Nay, would I were so anger'd with the same!
O hateful hands, to tear such loving words!
Injurious wasps, to feed on such sweet honey
And kill the bees that yield it with your stings!
I'll kiss each several paper for amends.
Look, here is writ "kind Julia." Unkind Julia!
As in revenge of thy ingratitude,
I throw thy name against the bruising stones,
Trampling contemptuously on thy disdain.
And here is writ "love-wounded Proteus."
Poor wounded name! My bosom as a bed
Shall lodge thee till thy wound be thoroughly heal'd;
And thus I search it with a sovereign kiss.
But twice or thrice was "Proteus" written down.
Be calm, good wind, blow not a word away
Till I have found each letter in the letter,
Except mine own name: that some whirlwind bear
Unto a ragged, fearful-hanging rock,
And throw it thence into the raging sea!
Lo, here in one line is his name twice writ,
"Poor forlorn Proteus, passionate Proteus,
To the sweet Julia."—That I'll tear away.
And yet I will not, sith so prettily

He couples it to his complaining names.
Thus will I fold them one on another:
Now kiss, embrace, contend, do what you will.

Launce: "Nay, 'twill be this hour ere I have done weeping" [Act II, Scene 3]

{Launce, the servant of lovesick Proteus, has his own problems with the hard-hearted dog Crab, who has betrayed no sadness at Launce's departure.}

Nay, 'twill be this hour ere I have done weeping. All the kind of the Launces have this very fault. I have received my proportion, like the prodigious son, and am going with Sir Proteus to the Imperial's court. I think Crab, my dog, be the sourest-natured dog that lives. My mother weeping, my father wailing, my sister crying, our maid howling, our cat wringing her hands, and all our house in a great perplexity, yet did not this cruel-hearted cur shed one tear. He is a stone, a very pebble stone, and has no more pity in him than a dog. A Jew would have wept to have seen our parting. Why, my grandam, having no eyes, look you, wept herself blind at my parting. Nay, I'll show you the manner of it. This shoe is my father. No, this left shoe is my father. No, no, this left shoe is my mother. Nay, that cannot be so neither. Yes, it is so, it is so, it hath the worser sole. This shoe, with the hole in it, is my mother, and this my father. A vengeance on't! There 'tis. Now, sir, this staff is my sister, for, look you, she is as white as a lily and as small as a wand. This hat is Nan, our maid. I am the dog. No, the dog is himself, and I am the dog.—O, the dog is me, and I am myself. Ay, so, so. Now come I to my father. Father, your blessing. Now should not the shoe speak a word for weeping. Now should I kiss my father; well, he weeps on. Now come I to my mother. O, that she could speak now like a wood woman! Well, I kiss her; why, there 'tis. Here's my mother's breath up and down. Now come I to my sister; mark the moan she makes. Now the dog all this while sheds not a tear nor speaks a word, but see how I lay the dust with my tears.

Proteus: "To leave my Julia, shall I be forsworn"
[Act II, Scene 6]

{*A gentleman of Verona, Proteus, having forsaken his beloved Julia for Silvia, whom his friend Valentine loves, is in a dilemma.*}

To leave my Julia, shall I be forsworn;
To love fair Silvia, shall I be forsworn;
To wrong my friend, I shall be much forsworn;
And even that power which gave me first my oath
Provokes me to this threefold perjury.
Love bade me swear and Love bids me forswear.
O sweet-suggesting Love, if thou hast sinned,
Teach me, thy tempted subject, to excuse it!
At first I did adore a twinkling star,
But now I worship a celestial sun.
Unheedful vows may heedfully be broken,
And he wants wit that wants resolvèd will
To learn his wit t' exchange the bad for better.
Fie, fie, unreverend tongue, to call her bad,
Whose sovereignty so oft thou hast preferr'd
With twenty thousand soul-confirming oaths!
I cannot leave to love, and yet I do;
But there I leave to love where I should love.
Julia I lose and Valentine I lose:
If I keep them, I needs must lose myself;
If I lose them, thus find I by their loss:
For Valentine, myself; for Julia, Silvia.
I to myself am dearer than a friend,
For love is still most precious in itself;
And Silvia—witness Heaven, that made her fair!—
Shows Julia but a swarthy Ethiope.
I will forget that Julia is alive,
Remembering that my love to her is dead;
And Valentine I'll hold an enemy,
Aiming at Silvia as a sweeter friend.
I cannot now prove constant to myself,
Without some treachery used to Valentine.
This night he meaneth with a corded ladder

To climb celestial Silvia's chamber-window,
Myself in counsel, his competitor.
Now presently I'll give her father notice
Of their disguising and pretended flight;
Who, all enraged, will banish Valentine;
For Thurio, he intends, shall wed his daughter;
But, Valentine being gone, I'll quickly cross
By some sly trick blunt Thurio's dull proceeding.
Love, lend me wings to make my purpose swift,
As thou hast lent me wit to plot this drift!

Valentine: "And why not death rather than living torment?" [Act III, Scene 1]

{*Valentine, the other gentleman of Verona, loves Silvia, and she loves him. Her father, the Duke of Milan, hopes to marry her to someone else, however, and, having discovered Valentine's intentions, has ordered him out of Milan.*}

And why not death rather than living torment?
To die is to be banish'd from myself.
And Silvia is myself: banish'd from her
Is self from self: a deadly banishment!
What light is light, if Silvia be not seen?
What joy is joy, if Silvia be not by?
Unless it be to think that she is by
And feed upon the shadow of perfection.
Except I be by Silvia in the night,
There is no music in the nightingale;
Unless I look on Silvia in the day,
There is no day for me to look upon.
She is my essence, and I leave to be,
If I be not by her fair influence
Foster'd, illumin'd, cherish'd, kept alive.
I fly not death to fly his deadly doom:
Tarry I here, I but attend on death:
But, fly I hence, I fly away from life.

Launce: "When a man's servant shall play the cur with him, look you, it goes hard . . ." [Act IV, Scene 4]

{Launce reviews the sins and ingratitude of his dog Crab.}

When a man's servant shall play the cur with him, look you, it goes hard: one that I brought up of a puppy; one that I saved from drowning, when three or four of his blind brothers and sisters went to it. I have taught him, even as one would say precisely, "Thus I would teach a dog." I was sent to deliver him as a present to Mistress Silvia from my master; and I came no sooner into the dining-chamber but he steps me to her trencher and steals her capon's leg. O, 'tis a foul thing when a cur cannot keep himself in all companies! I would have, as one should say, one that takes upon him to be a dog indeed, to be, as it were, a dog at all things. If I had not had more wit than he, to take a fault upon me that he did, I think verily he had been hanged for't. Sure as I live, he had suffered for't. You shall judge. He thrusts me himself into the company of three or four gentlemanlike dogs under the duke's table. He had not been there—bless the mark!—a pissing while, but all the chamber smelt him. "Out with the dog!" says one. "What cur is that?" says another. "Whip him out," says the third. "Hang him up," says the duke. I, having been acquainted with the smell before, knew it was Crab, and goes me to the fellow that whips the dogs. "Friend," quoth I, "you mean to whip the dog?" "Ay, marry, do I," quoth he. "You do him the more wrong," quoth I; " 'twas I did the thing you wot of." He makes me no more ado, but whips me out of the chamber. How many masters would do this for his servant? Nay, I'll be sworn, I have sat in the stocks for puddings he hath stolen, otherwise he had been executed. I have stood on the pillory for geese he hath killed, otherwise he had suffered for't. Thou thinkest not of this now. Nay, I remember the trick you served me when I took my leave of Madam Silvia. Did not I bid thee still mark me and do as I do? When didst thou see me heave up my leg and make water against a gentlewoman's farthingale? Didst thou ever see me do such a trick?

Julia: "A virtuous gentlewoman, mild and beautiful"
[Act IV, Scene 4]

{*Julia, who loves Proteus, has come to Milan after him. In disguise as his new servant Sebastian, she goes to his new beloved, Silvia, with a ring, which Silvia exchanges for a portrait. Upon leaving Julia compares and contrasts herself with her rival.*}

A virtuous gentlewoman, mild and beautiful.
I hope my master's suit will be but cold,
Since she respects my mistress' love so much.
Alas, how love can trifle with itself!
Here is her picture. Let me see; I think,
If I had such a tire, this face of mine
Were full as lovely as is this of hers:
And yet the painter flatter'd her a little,
Unless I flatter with myself too much.
Her hair is auburn, mine is perfect yellow:
If that be all the difference in his love,
I'll get me such a colour'd periwig.
Her eyes are grey as glass, and so are mine:
Ay, but her forehead's low, and mine's as high.
What should it be that he respects in her
But I can make respective in myself,
If this fond Love were not a blinded god?
Come, shadow, come and take this shadow up,
For 'tis thy rival. O thou senseless form,
Thou shalt be worshipped, kissed, loved, and adored!
And, were there sense in his idolatry,
My substance should be statue in thy stead.
I'll use thee kindly for thy mistress' sake,
That used me so; or else, by Jove I vow,
I should have scratch'd out your unseeing eyes
To make my master out of love with thee!

Valentine: "How use doth breed a habit in a man!"
[Act V, Scene 4]

{*Valentine, having in banishment from Milan taken up the captainship of some gentlemanly outlaws, has not gotten over his Silvia, who (he does not know yet) has just been discovered by his crew.*}

How use doth breed a habit in a man!
This shadowy desert, unfrequented woods,
I better brook than flourishing peopled towns:
Here can I sit alone, unseen of any,
And to the nightingale's complaining notes
Tune my distresses and record my woes.
O thou that dost inhabit in my breast,
Leave not the mansion so long tenantless,
Lest, growing ruinous, the building fall
And leave no memory of what it was!
Repair me with thy presence, Silvia.
Thou gentle nymph, cherish thy forlorn swain!

[*He hears shouting close by.*]

What halloing and what stir is this today?
These are my mates, that make their wills their law,
Have some unhappy passenger in chase.
They love me well; yet I have much to do
To keep them from uncivil outrages.
Withdraw thee, Valentine. Who's this comes here?

THE WINTER'S TALE

Camillo: "O miserable lady! But, for me" [Act I, Scene 2]

{*A young lord of Sicilia, Camillo, has been ordered by his king Leontes to murder the king of Bohemia, Polixenes, who Leontes rashly believes has slept with his queen. Camillo, disbelieving in Queen Hermione's guilt, but unable to dissuade the mad Leontes from his murderous whim, sees what he must do.*}

O miserable lady! But, for me,
What case stand I in? I must be the poisoner
Of good Polixenes; and my ground to do't
Is the obedience to a master, one
Who in rebellion with himself will have
All that are his so too. To do this deed,
Promotion follows. If I could find example
Of thousands that had struck anointed kings
And flourish'd after, I'd not do't; but since
Nor brass nor stone nor parchment bears not one,
Let villainy itself forswear't. I must
Forsake the court. To do't, or no, is certain
To me a break-neck. Happy star, reign now!
Here comes Bohemia.